BECOMING MINDSET

BECOMING MINDSET

TURNING PAIN INTO POWER

BRENDAN BARBATO

NEW DEGREE PRESS

COPYRIGHT © 2021 BRENDAN BARBATO

BECOMING MINDSET
Turning Pain into Power

ISBN   978-1-63676-733-8 *Paperback*
          978-1-63730-034-3 *Kindle Ebook*
          978-1-63730-136-4 *Ebook*

To my life partner, Eiko.

CONTENTS

―――――

INTRODUCTION

———

I was diagnosed as a type 1 diabetic when I was two years old. My glucose level was over 1,000 mg/dL, and I could have easily gone into a coma or died. Throughout the past twenty-three years of my life, my health journey has been riddled with stomach pain, chronic insomnia, sports injuries, and surgery for my breathing, which resulted in fourteen hospitalizations and over two hundred doctor's visits.

Despite all of these challenges, when you look at me you will see a "regular" person who loves to travel, is married, and works his butt off every day—not someone with a disability. It took me years to gain the courage to share my story; I was afraid it would make my situation worse because I was worried about what people might think. After graduating from college, I started to think about how I wanted to spend the rest of my life. After reflecting, the decision was to care less about what people expected me to do and to focus on owning my own narrative. Being authentic and vulnerable by sharing my hidden, internal pain ultimately made me stronger because I no longer internalized negative thoughts.

Ultimately, my story has many similarities to people globally. In the United States alone, the CDC reported that six in ten adults have a chronic disease, and four in ten adults have two or more.[1] These are your family members, neighbors, and people from your community. You might feel comfortable sharing your story with your doctor, but what about your friends?

I posted online to recruit interviews for this book. A friend tagged Emily Lemiska as a good fit, and after our conversation, I saw why. Emily has Klippel-Feil syndrome (KFS), which causes severe spinal pain and was a result of missing vertebral discs. In Emily's case, she was missing six. Despite her eventual diagnosis, Emily grew up healthy, excelled in school, and played sports like volleyball. Overtime, Emily noticed she had a short neck and started to become self-conscious of her appearance, but her doctors told her she would be fine. In fact, she would not be fine. Emily's KFS caused years of pain, suffering, and coming to terms with the devastating truth that there was no cure. Then she did something magical. She built a relationship with her illness.

After speaking with and learning from Emily's resilience and strength, my view of pain changed dramatically. I needed to learn more, which led to dozens of interviews to try and understand how people—chronically ill or healthy—deal with and take control of their pain.

---

1   "Chronic Disease in America," National Center for Chronic Disease Prevention and Health Promotion, accessed October 6, 2020.

When I started interviewing and researching, it became clear that people were afraid to share information or open up to me about their health. A 2016 study by the National Institute of Health on how patients communicate about their illnesses stated, "Some patients choose not to share health information to reduce burdens on family members, though these preferences may change overtime."[2] We are our own worst critics and assume that we are a burden and that no one wants to help.

However, Civic Science polled two thousand US adults based on their comfort of asking for help and concluded that "individuals underestimate the likelihood that someone will help them by as much as 50 percent, meaning that people are far more willing to help than we may assume."[3]

I completely understand why people do not want to share their pain with others. Sharing your story makes you vulnerable, but being comfortable with yourself allows you to be strong because you start to own your narrative. No matter where you are in this journey, it is important to think about how sharing your story can impact your mental health and well-being.

While this book highlights the American perspective, an article by the Canadian Mental Health Association set out to understand how mental illnesses and chronic physical conditions coexist and found that "biology, illness experience,

---

2   Catherin Lim et al., "'It just seems outside my health': How Patients with Chronic Conditions Perceive Communication Boundaries with Providers," *Designing Interactive Systems (Conference)* 2016 (2016): 1172–184.

3   Laurnie Wilson, "Asking for Help May Be a Privilege," *CivicScience*, September 13, 2018.

and social determinants of health can increase the likelihood of someone living with a mental illness or chronic physical condition developing a co-existing condition."[4]

The problem with treating chronic mental or physical health is that we are taught to overcome our struggle. But I have a different belief. Your pain and struggle become a part of you. Basically, if you live with a mental health condition, you have a higher likelihood of developing a chronic illness and vice versa.

The lessons of this book are valuable regardless of if you have a chronic illness or not. Ultimately, this book contains insights into how to help yourself and others. Plus, there is a deep emphasis on building mental strength regardless of what stage of your life you are in.

After reflecting on my own situation, as well as research and interviews with some incredible individuals, a few of the strategies that help those with a chronic illness grow stronger are:

1. Focus on building a relationship with your chronic illness rather than overcoming it. In the case of diabetes, I cannot be cured, so the battle is daily. Focus on managing your health and making smart decisions.
2. Explore alternative approaches to traditional medicines instead of prescriptions, shots, and surgeries. Meditation,

---

4   "The Relationship between Mental Health, Mental Illness and Chronic Physical Conditions," Canadian Mental Health Association, accessed October 6, 2020.

yoga, and acupuncture can go a long way for stress and tension.

3. Find your community of people who listen, can relate, and are willing to lend a hand.

4. Share your story because internalizing pain and stress can be harmful to your mental health and relationships.

Becoming Mindset is an approach to harness hidden pain, suffering, or illness to realize your true potential. Utilize these stories to give you strength on your journey from pain to feeling well. Whether it is my personal struggle with diabetes, Emily and her spinal surgery, or the other individuals mentioned in this book, we are going to explore the Becoming Mindset and how these mental shifts can increase your health and happiness.

The information presented has been written with *you* in mind. No matter your personal struggle.

Sharing my own experiences will hopefully show that you are not alone, inspire you to share your own story, and help you improve your personal health and wellness.

This journey is divided into three separate parts:

Part 1: How We Got Here and My Personal Story
Part 2: Becoming Mindset: The Seven Principles.
Part 3: Embracing the Becoming Mindset: Children, Adults, and Support Roles.

Please remember, the Becoming Mindset is an ongoing process, and I hope you embark on this journey with me.

PART I

CHAPTER 1

A DEFINING DIAGNOSIS

─────

THE DIAGNOSIS THAT CHANGED MY LIFE

I was only two years old when it happened. After days of
battling wet diapers, dehydration, and weight loss, my
parents rushed me to the doctor. On March 14, 1998, I was
diagnosed with type 1 diabetes. A blood test revealed that
my blood glucose level was over 1,000 mg/dL. I could have
easily entered into a coma or died.

I was immediately sent to Hasbro Children's Hospital in
Providence, Rhode Island, because a glucose level over 125
mg/dL means you are at risk of diabetes, and mine was eight
times higher. A high reading means sugar was entering my
urine and that I could enter diabetic ketoacidosis (DKA),
which is a buildup of acid in my blood and can be lethal. To
avoid DKA, I was admitted to the pediatric intensive care
unit (PICU).

My parents were shocked at how young I developed type
1 diabetes, but I was not alone. Over forty thousand type 1
diabetics are diagnosed each year in the United States. My

parents adjusted to this news and grew strong, becoming my full-time caregivers until I took over at fifteen years old.[5] They listened to my doctors and met with diabetes educators to learn how to count carbohydrates, monitor symptoms, and inject syringes.

My earliest memory, still clear in my mind today, is from this first hospital visit. The nurse wheeled me around in a red wagon, where I sat in the warmth of my quilted blanket with teddy bears. Despite how comfortable I was, nothing could have prepared me for what waited around the final corner. Another nurse stood waiting to inject insulin into my arm. She raised the syringe, sucked the insulin out with the needle, flicked the syringe to expel air bubbles, squeezed out two units, and then plunged the needle into my skin. I cried. To this day, I inject an average of six needles per day to keep me alive.

Overnight, my parents became diabetes experts. The only thing that stopped me from going home was maintaining a stable glucose level. I needed a few days of consistent readings, but on the first day, the doctor only got them down to 466 mg/dL and eventually the 200s. Nondiabetics and even some type 2 diabetics create insulin naturally; therefore, calculating the right dosage is always a challenge, especially as you grow older and your body changes. You need to factor in what you are eating, the time of day, and a standard dosage that works. Every day demands constant monitoring to ensure I do not get sick, which requires a lifetime of trial and error to get right. After five days in the PICU, I finally went home.

---

5   "Diabetes: Facts, Statistics, and You", Healthline Media, Inc., accessed November 2, 2020.

Being diagnosed as a type 1 diabetic when I was two years old required me to be an adult from an early age. If I felt lightheaded or sick and did not speak up, it could result in an unnecessary hospital visit. The only time I find myself reminded of my diabetes, now, is when my glucose is too high or low. My wife often forgets I even am diabetic, because of how well I take care of my health.

HOW I MANAGE (MONITOR) MY DIABETES

As a type 1 diabetic, I still live a happy and productive life. Every time I leave my house, I carry an insulin pen, needles, alcohol pads, and my cell phone to track my glucose results. Also, every two weeks, I insert a Dexcom continuous glucose monitor in my abdomen, which sends my glucose reading to my phone every five minutes. Managing diabetes can be a lot of work, but the better I take care of myself, the more freedom and independence I have.

I refuse to let my diabetes define what I can and cannot do. If I want to play soccer, I am going to play soccer. If I want to travel the world, I will. To ensure I can live the life I want to, I constantly research new strategies for managing not only my diabetes but my mental health as it can be difficult to stay positive when you feel sick. Having a chronic illness might be life-altering, but with the right mindset, anyone can still achieve whatever they desire.

That said, learning to manage my diabetes has been a journey. As I grew up, I quickly became in charge of all decisions, which meant each action was up to me. The way I maintain my health now is far different than how I handled my well-being when I was younger.

When I was a child, treatments were more archaic. In the past, a diabetic used syringes and vials of insulin that required an ice pack when traveling as well as a glucose monitoring set. Sleepovers were difficult with all my "processes," so my house became the hangout spot. If I spent the night at my friends' house, my mom had to stop by in the morning to give me an insulin injection. It was not until I was fifteen that I finally felt comfortable and confident enough to manage my own diabetic care. All it took was one mistake for me to end up in the hospital, and that fear controlled me until I gave myself the first injection.

One year, I fell out of a bouncy castle at my own birthday party and almost passed out. My glucose was 28 mg/dL, and anything below 40 mg/dL is incredibly dangerous. The lowest I have ever seen my glucose was 19 mg/dL when I fell in a parking lot and my grandparents fed me donuts and sugar packets to keep me from passing out. Both of these instances were rare, but once the situation was resolved, I was right back in the castle or in the car with nothing more than a small stomach ache from consuming too much sugar at once.

Now, I travel the world so long as I have my insulin. In May of 2019, I was promoted to a global role that required me to travel to cities around the world such as Berlin, Paris, and Tel Aviv. Having visited fifteen countries and over fifty cities, I have rarely had issues. I am always on high alert, making sure I feel well, and if something goes wrong, I am not afraid to ask for help. One time I accidentally left my insulin in the pocket of the pants I placed inside of a washing machine in Paris. I called my insurance company, found a doctor, got a local prescription, and kept pushing forward.

Monitoring diabetes is just another task in my life, like brushing my teeth or taking out the trash—the stakes are just higher. If I want to eat something, I inject the right amount of insulin. When I am wrong, I correct and learn. If I want to travel or exercise, I monitor my glucose levels closely and keep pushing ahead until I need to stop, likely when my symptoms of high or low glucose start.

SO, WHAT IS DIABETES?

Diabetes is a highly misunderstood disease. One in ten Americans have been diagnosed with either type 1 or type 2 diabetes, and one in three Americans have prediabetes (88 million people).[6] Because the majority of Americans are diabetic or at risk of diabetes, I really want to discuss the different types in depth and clarify common misconceptions, especially since type 2 is preventable in many cases.

In simple terms, type 1 diabetes is an autoimmune disease in which your pancreas does not create insulin, which is necessary for survival. On the other hand, type 2 diabetes is a metabolic condition, meaning the body does not produce enough insulin or has resistance to it—typically due to lifestyle choices or being overweight.

The cause of type 1 diabetes, let alone a cure, is unknown. For type 2, however, if you change your lifestyle and diet, you can often reverse the condition and go back to living your life. Below is an overview of the disease:

---

6   O'Neill, Hayes, Tara, Josee Farmer, "Insulin Cost and Pricing Trends," *American Action Forum*, April 2, 2020

Differences between Type 1 and Type 2 Diabetes[7]

	Type 1 Diabetes	Type 2 Diabetes
Characterization	Autoimmune disease, meaning the immune system attacks the beta cells in the pancreas, which stops the pancreas from creating insulin	Metabolic condition, meaning the pancreas no longer produces enough insulin or is resistant to it. The pancreas functions, but not as well as it should.
Cause	Autoimmune disease	Metabolic condition
Age of Diagnosis	Typically as a child	Typically as an adult
Prevention	There is no prevention because the cause is still unknown.	Genetics can play a part but typically is preventable by living an active, healthy lifestyle.
Treatment	Insulin injections and constant glucose monitoring	Lifestyle changes, diet, exercise, and potentially pills/insulin
Insulin Production	No insulin production. Without insulin, organs will shut down and lead to death.	Some insulin but can regain creation through diet and exercise
Risk Factor	Family members who have type 1 diabetes, genetics, and environmental factors	Genetics, lifestyle choices, and being overweight
US Diabetic Population (2018)[8]	1.6 million	32.6 million

7   "National Diabetes Statistics Report 2020," Centers for Disease Control and Prevention, US Department of Health & Human Services, accessed November 2, 2020.

8   "Number of Americans with Diabetes Projected to Double or Triple by 2050," Centers for Disease Control and Prevention, accessed November 2, 2020.

Even if you are not diabetic, you likely know someone who is. Medical research has come a long way in the last century, but if current diagnosis trends continue, one in three US adults could have diabetes by 2050.[9] On the other hand, without the invention of insulin in 1921 by Frederick Banting, anyone with type 1 diabetes might not live more than forty-eight hours, because without insulin, your organs will fail.[10]

Learning about the many ways diabetes can complicate your life if not controlled makes me cheer for people like Dr. Denise Faustman, the director of Massachusetts General Hospital's Immunobiology Lab. Dr. Faustman has an ambitious goal: cure diabetes. Curing a chronic disease like diabetes, Crohn's, cancer, or Lyme is not easy, but anything is possible. Like Dr. Faustman says, "Diabetes didn't occur in a day, and maybe the reversal doesn't occur in a day."[11] I am realistic in believing that a cure for diabetes will take time, but I am hopeful this disease will one day be cured—whether it impacts my life or the lives of future generations.

---

9   "National Diabetes Statistics Report 2020," Centers for Disease Control and Prevention, US Department of Health & Human Services, accessed November 2, 2020.

10 "The History of a Wonderful Thing We Call Insulin," American Diabetes Association, accessed November 2, 2020.

11 Alexandra Sifferlin, "There's Hope for a Vaccine to Prevent Type 1 Diabetes," *Time*, June 21, 2018.

DIABETES IS MY STRENGTH

Many people see diabetes as an incurable disease that weakens my body. I see diabetes as a major strength. It makes you a resilient fighter who sees pain as an obstacle but not a wall and much more cognizant of your own health and the health of those around you. Growing up, I never viewed myself as different or a diabetic. I was just a kid who took a break for a snack to raise sugar levels or to inject some insulin but then got right back to being a kid.

When I was young, I had to pay close attention to my health and understand that every action had a consequence. I always felt that way unintentionally, but as I matured, it became something I constantly thought about. There were times when I would think, "If I play soccer for two hours, should I eat a large snack beforehand to avoid a low glucose reading that can make me lightheaded or even pass out?" One of the worst experiences was having to raise my hand in the middle of class to go to the nurse because I am an introvert and interrupting class made me anxious.

When I was twelve years old, one of my highlights was winning the state championships in penalty kicks and successfully scoring the third goal. My lowlight was a couple of years later when my glucose went low during tryouts for the "A team." I stopped, drank juice and ate crackers, and was playing fifteen minutes later. The coach thought this was an issue because if it happened during a game, I would be a liability to the team. He cut me.

I could have backed down and accepted the circumstances, but I refused to stop fighting and making progress. I might have made the "B team," but I was on such a mission to beat his team in scrimmages, and I even scored four goals on his son—the goalie—which felt empowering. I did not make the team that year, but I made the team every single year going forward because I trained relentlessly.

Ultimately, growing up with diabetes made me become an adult more quickly because of my responsibilities and required discipline. There were, and still are, no days off.

As one of my favorite authors, Viktor Frankl, states, "Forces beyond your control can take away everything you possess except one thing, your freedom to choose how you will respond to the situation." Being diagnosed with an illness or disease that might never be cured can be defeating, but when I started to view my diabetes as a strength and not a weakness, I felt motivated to take control of my health and well-being.

I constantly have to pay attention to my life, and this will happen daily until there is a cure. Maintaining my diabetes has allowed me to likely live a longer, better life as I age rather than one with damaged nerves and organs. Growing up, there was a lot of room for improvement, but at twenty-five-years old, I am in control of my disease. It took twenty-three years to get to this point, and it would have happened much faster if I adopted the Becoming Mindset sooner.

ACTIONS & REFLECTIONS

1. Reflect and note something you did recently that caused you pain. Was it a one-time issue, or will it happen again? Each action has a consequence, so what can you do to maintain your wellness?

2. Make a list of 5–10 areas of your life that are in your control and how you can improve—for example, exercising daily or tracking your diet.

3. Write down five positive achievements you made recently. Celebrate the positives in your life.

CHAPTER 2

HISTORY OF HEALTHCARE

———

Whether you have a chronic illness, know someone with a chronic illness, or thought "Hey, this book will be useful to my life," you need to understand how we got here. I have been a diabetic for twenty-three years, and I am always amazed by how much progress we have made in certain areas and how far behind we are in others.

We might have read about SARS in 2003, H1N1 swine flu in 2009, or the bubonic plague of 1334 that killed twenty-five million people and a third of Europe.[12] COVID-19 taught us how an invisible virus can close international borders and economies with ease.

So, what do plagues have to do with chronic illnesses? Well, plagues show the journey of medicine and how cultural

---

12   Jenny, Howard, "Plague was one of history's deadliest diseases—then we found a cure," *National Geographic*, July 6, 2020.

and environmental shifts have either helped or worsened chronic illnesses. The best place to begin understanding chronic illnesses is through life expectancy, which is a solid measure of how we are progressing from a medical and cultural standpoint.

In 2019, the global life expectancy was 72.6 years due to rapid advancements in health, research, and new technologies.[13] Despite people living longer, many problems still exist. The website of Blue Cross Blue Shield states that "Health care spending in the United States is $3 trillion a year, straining the budgets of families, businesses, and taxpayers alike."[14] A country full of chronically ill people is expensive. The website also states that access to health care, better nutrition, and financial stability lead to less stress and a more livable environment.

Blue Cross Blue Shield states there are three key factors driving US health care costs: prescription drugs, chronic illnesses, and our lifestyle. They predict prescription drug prices to increase by 136 percent between 2010 and 2025. Treating chronic diseases accounts for 86 percent of US health care costs, and "Americans' unhealthy lifestyle choices are linked to costly chronic conditions."[15] We are in dire need of change.

---

13   Max Roser et al., "Life Expectancy," *Our World in Data*, October 2019.

14   "Why does healthcare cost so much?" Blue Cross Blue Shield, accessed November 10, 2020

15   "Why does healthcare cost so much?" Blue Cross Blue Shield, accessed November 10, 2020

THE ECONOMICS OF A CHRONIC ILLNESS

As of 2017, the United States spends $3.5 trillion on health expenditures, which is 17.9 percent of gross domestic product.[16] Looking at just one chronic illness, diabetes impacts 10 percent of US adults today, and this figure is expected to grow to 20 percent in 2025 and 33 percent in 2050.[17] Without intervention, diabetes puts you at high risk for a heart attack, stroke, blindness, kidney failure, and loss of toes, feet, or legs. Without the right lifestyle choices, you are likely putting your long-term health at risk.

As a type 1 diabetic, I have to constantly make financial decisions in relation to my health. Insurance is important for unpredictable expenses, yet, as of 2019, 26.1 million Americans did not have health insurance.[18] The archaic supplies I used to use—a finger prick and blood test strip—are covered by insurance, but my Dexcom glucose monitor costs me approximately $100 per month, even with insurance. If health insurance companies focused on the long-term, they might even save money since I would require less medical attention. We all win. But that's not how it works.

The cost of health care makes us question if an ambulance ride or a surgery is worth the debt it can cause. In fact, one in four Americans is skipping medical care because of cost.[19]

---

16 "Health Expenditures," Centers for Disease Control and Prevention, accessed November 10, 2020.

17 "About Prediabetes & Type 2 Diabetes," Centers for Disease Control and Prevention, accessed November 10, 2020.

18 Katherine, Keisler-Starkey, et al., "Health Insurance Coverage in the United States: 2019." *United States Census Bureau*, September 15, 2020

19 Megan Leonhardt, "Nearly 1 in 4 Americans are Skipping Medical Care Because of the Cost," *CNBC*, March 12 2020.

Conditions such as heart failure can cost you $51,937, and who has that kind of money saved for a rainy day? You are not only sick but potentially one of the 32 percent of American workers who have medical debt.[20] Until we have a health care system that puts people over profit, patients will likely struggle to get the health care they need because it is unaffordable.

While I do not know how to fix the US health care system entirely, I recently had an experience that gave me a sense of hope. In September of 2019, I was in Munich, Germany, for a work trip. I became ill and needed to see a doctor, so I spoke to our business insurance firm and was connected to an international clinic at the Munich train station. I was uninsured in Germany and paid the doctor directly out of pocket. After being diagnosed with bronchitis, I paid the doctor the equivalent of US$50 and another US$15 for my medications. Meanwhile, in the United States, the average physician visit is $265.[21] The antibiotic would cost another $20.[22]

Germany has mandatory health care, and despite being a foreigner, I felt taken care of.[23] So why is the United States' health care experience so terrible? I believe it is because we

20   "32% of American Workers Have Medical Debt—and Over Half Have Defaulted On it," CNBC, accessed October 10, 2020.

21   Steven R. Machlin, et al. "Expenses for Office-Based Physician Visits by Specialty and Insurance Type 2016." Agency for Healthcare Research and Quality. October 2018.

22   "How Much Do Antibiotics Cost Without Insurance?" RxSaver, accessed November 10, 2020.

23   "Health Care in Germany: The German Health Care System," Institute for Quality and Efficiency in Health Care 2006

are less focused on cures and more focused on disease management. We need a patient-centric system.

DISEASE MANAGEMENT, NOT CURES

Since 1945, only 3 percent of pharmaceutical inventions were cures—consisting primarily of antibiotics—and the remaining 97 percent were all medications.[24] Has technology reached its limit, or is there a lack of incentives for cures? Well, we have fighter jets, we can send text messages around the world in real time, and we have been to the moon, so my guess is the technology can get there but the incentives are misaligned.

The United States is capitalistic which is somewhat understandable, but a healthier population leads to a more productive economy. More sick people are only better for pharmaceutical companies, doctors, and hospitals. For example, let's look at heart disease and strokes, which kill more Americans than any other cause or disease. Combined, they cost the United States health care system $214 billion per year *and* $138 billion in lost productivity.[25]

While finding a cure for cancer, diabetes, or heart disease is a grueling task, the speed at which pharmaceutical companies are moving to launch a vaccine to stop the COVID-19 pandemic proves it can happen. On average, vaccine development

---

24   *TEDxTalks*, "Ashkan Fardost: A Cure for No Cure: The Next Generation of Medicine," October 14, 2015, video, 14:17.

25   "Health and Economic Costs of Chronic Diseases," Centers for Disease Control and Prevention, accessed November 10, 2020.

takes 10–15 years.[26] Pharmaceutical companies are receiving large government contracts and see a huge business opportunity in vaccinating not only Americans but people globally. Their timeline to have a vaccine is not 10–15 years but 10–15 months, and scientists made it happen. So why stop at solving COVID-19?

As of 2021, doctors are disease managers. Between "60–80 percent of primary care doctor visits are related to stress, yet only 3 percent of patients receive stress management help."[27] If your knee hurts, an orthopedist will ask you what makes it worse and what helps. Doctors are excellent at solving surface level pain like a broken finger or a cold, but deeper problems, such as chronic illness, require a lot more effort.

Understanding and diagnosing chronic illness calls for countless tests, typically more than one doctor, and a whole lot of patience. Beyond tests, doctors need to understand your stress level, work–life balance, and numerous other questions before deciding if you have a chronic illness and what the next steps are. In medicine, it is a game of trial and error. Try the most likely solution and keep trying the next remedy until you start making progress. I have empathy for doctors, too, because this takes patience and time.

To become a doctor, it takes four years of undergraduate study, four years of medical school, and another three to

---

26   "Vaccine Development, Testing and Regulation," The History of Vaccines, accessed November 10, 2020.

27   "How Stress Affects the Body," HeartMath, accessed November 10, 2020.

seven years in residency depending on your specialty.[28] Despite all of the education, doctors are resources, not the decision makers. You are in control of your body. We need to use doctors as a resource to help enhance our well-being because only you feel the impact of your treatment decision— not your doctor.

Unfortunately, we cannot all receive the support that professional athletes do. Players have a team doctor, trainers, physical therapists, therapists, and more. LeBron James, my favorite NBA player, spends $1.5 million per year to take care of his body.[29] He does whatever it takes to win, and the investment in his body gives him the best chance. However, as you will learn in parts II and III of this book, you do not have to be a millionaire to be healthy and feel well. There are numerous ways you can either prevent chronic illness or get to a point where you feel well despite not being healthy.

You have to be in charge of your life, or other people will continue making decisions for you. The best way to treat your body is to get out in front of pain. Stretch before you exercise, get your eight hours of sleep, and, above all, avoid reactive measures like painkillers and surgery.

---

28   "Becoming a Doctor in the US: Medical School, Residency & Licensing Requirements," Study.com, accessed November 10, 2020.

29   Scott Davis, "LeBron James Reportedly Spends $1.5 Million Per Year To Take Care of His Body," *Business Insider*, July 29, 2018

EDUCATION DRIVES AWARENESS

Have you ever had someone look at you and utter the words, "You don't look sick?" It is one of the most annoying things that anyone can say to someone with a chronic illness. What you might see externally is far different from how I feel internally. I have seen athletes in top shape who are constantly down on themselves, while I know people who are in a wheelchair who are the most positive people you will ever meet. Do not judge a book by its cover.

One time in San Francisco, I was on the train to work. It was packed, and there were multiple open seats in the handicapped section. I took a seat. Diabetes is an invisible disability, but I was also going through physical therapy and had immense back pain. Within minutes, an older couple told me I looked fine and that I was not allowed to sit there. I made eye contact, got up, and stood in pain while I held the support strap while the train swayed around turns. I wish I stood up for myself at that moment, and I certainly would now. The fact that I look pretty damn good (Ha!) does not at all reflect what I am feeling or the internal pain I am fighting.

Kevin Hoegler, whose personal story appears in chapter 13, had a similar experience during COVID. If you meet Kevin, he is one of the fittest people you will ever see. He runs daily, goes to the gym, and is relatively healthy, but he has multiple sclerosis (MS). Kevin's MS is mostly under control, but unpredictable episodes cause muscle weakness, balance challenges, tingling numbness, and more. It can be debilitating. However, while Kevin might have MS, MS does not have him.

During COVID, Kevin was going to the grocery store in the early morning. Like most stores during the COVID pandemic, they had specific hours for those who are at risk—the elderly, disabled, etc. Kevin approached the grocery store, and the staff asked Kevin to prove he had MS because he looked healthy. Why does he have to prove he has MS? Why would he lie about that? Kevin was heartbroken and went home, but he wanted to turn a negative moment into a positive learning experience. He knew the staff was just ignorant of what MS was, and he was happy the incident happened to him and not someone else—because he could handle the outcome.

Kevin's goal was to educate the grocery staff, so he spoke with the local MS organization in New Jersey to ensure that no one else experienced what he did. I admire him deeply for this because it would have been so easy to run, never go to this store again, and build up negative thoughts around these types of unfortunate situations. The more we build awareness, the less this will happen.

When you see someone who is going for a run, navigating in a wheelchair, or whatever it may be, never assume you understand their happiness. Everyone is battling something. The sooner we have this level of awareness and develop empathy for other human beings, the better our society will be. You have a voice, pain is not always visible, and the more we understand one another and communicate, the better off our world will be. More community and less judgment will create a more inclusive society.

ACTIONS & REFLECTIONS

1. Research your pain and see where it takes you. You might connect with nonprofits, read a medical research paper, or converse with people who can relate to your pain.

2. Become comfortable with the idea that you might always have pain, but it does not have you. Listen to your body, focusing on minimizing pain, inflammation, symptoms, and emphasizing prevention over reactive treatments.

3. Reflect on if there was a time when someone jumped to conclusions without knowing what you were going through. How did you feel? Don't take ignorance personally. Many people have no idea what you are going through. That is not your fault, so don't fight yourself internally.

CHAPTER 3

WHY OVERCOMING IS THE WRONG MINDSET

MENTAL ASPECT OF HEALTH

In her early twenties, my mom had a quarter of her stomach removed and was later diagnosed with Crohn's disease and irritable bowel syndrome (IBS). She had to start monitoring her diet and limiting stress to avoid a flare-up, which caused her an unbearable amount of pain throughout her body. As the Mayo Clinic states, "There is no one treatment [for Crohn's] that works for everyone. The goal of medical treatment is to reduce the inflammation that triggers your signs and symptoms."[30] Since there is no cure for Crohn's, the focus is on disease management. Adopting the right mindset will help you battle through the tough times and appreciate when things are going well.

---

30 "Crohn's Disease," Mayo Foundation for Medical Education and Research, accessed December 15, 2020.

When something negative happens in our lives, we often question what we did to deserve it. We look for a reason or a magic pill that will help us feel better. As mentioned in chapter 2, the relationship between mind and body is what sets the foundation for healing. The Canadian Mental Health Association confirms this by stating that "people living with a serious mental illness are at higher risk of experiencing a wide range of chronic physical conditions. Conversely, people with chronic physical health conditions experience depression and anxiety at twice the rate of the general population."[31] Therefore, we need to think of our body as an interconnected system.

In her talk "The Secret of Becoming Mentally Strong," psychologist Amy Morin discusses our unhealthy beliefs about ourselves, others, and the world.[32] One example is self-pity. This is toxic because of its emphasis on the problem, such as "Why does this always happen to me?" The solution is to reframe that thought into "I have the ability to control my life and health because, while people care about me, I have a responsibility to care about myself."

Another key area of being mentally strong is becoming patient. We live in a "takeout economy," where we want results yesterday. While your body has the ability to heal itself daily, progress takes effort and time. Healing requires strengthening your immune system through methods such

---

31 "The Relationship Between Mental Health, Mental Illness and Chronic Physical Conditions," Canadian Mental Health Association, accessed December 15, 2020.

32 *TEDxTalks*, "Amy Morin: The Secret to Becoming Mentally Strong," December 4, 2015, video.

as sleep. You might go to bed with an upset stomach and wake up feeling great. Boom. Healing. A study by Healthline found that when you do not get enough sleep during the wound healing process, your immune system becomes depleted, slowing down healing and putting you at risk for infection.[33] Feeling well takes time, effort, and patience.

Your mental health—stress, anxiety, depression, etc.—is important because it can negatively impact healing. Cuts will heal, but chronic diseases are managed because there is no cure. Once you learn that you cannot overcome chronic disease, you start to think about how you can enhance your quality of life and plan out how you can make that a reality. My recommendation is to build your ideal health plan and make changes based on trial and error. After you finish this book, you will be armed with the knowledge and resources to make this happen.

SURGERY ISN'T A CURE

When pain is prolonged, your nerves become not only more sensitive to pain signals but also more intense.[34] Surgery is often seen as a way to overcome your pain, but surgery is not a cure; it is a bandage. It might take six months to gain mobility after your knee surgery, your knee will be forever altered, and you might even need surgery again. Procedures also come with risks, including infection and medical error.

33 "How Sleep Deprivation Negatively Impacts Wound Healing," Advanced Tissue, accessed December 15, 2020.

34 Laura Kiesel, "Chronic Pain: The Invisible Disability." *Harvard Health Publishing* (blog). April 28, 2017.

Emily Lemiska just wanted her life back. Surgery for Emily's Klippel-Feil syndrome (KFS) was less of a choice and more a means of survival. Doctors were concerned that delaying the procedure could lead to irreversible nerve damage. Since there is no cure for KFS, Emily was focused on "overcoming" her symptoms through pain management. But was this the right mindset? Since KFS cannot be cured and is technically considered degenerative, could she truly overcome her chronic illness?

Emily had no reason to be optimistic, and yet she went into surgery reassuring herself that she would quickly recover. Her optimism likely came from her surgeon, who told Emily that she would be back to running in no time. Emily's surgery went well and her spinal cord was freed, but she was in excruciating pain and remained in the intensive care unit (ICU) for a week. Despite lying in bed hooked up to countless machines, Emily wholeheartedly believed the doctor when he said six weeks of recovery would make her feel better. He gave her hope.

To recover, Emily went to her family home in Connecticut where she could be best supported. "Recovery" consists of getting better overtime, but not for Emily. After two weeks, the pain was increasing. Emily realized that surgery might not have been the silver bullet she had anticipated, and, mentally, she struggled because there was no progress.

After a month and a half, it was time for Emily to go back to work. She dreaded going back to work with how bad she felt but adopted a fake-it-till-you-make-it mentality. While her employer was supportive and empathetic, there was only so much she could do at work without feeling depleted. Emily pushed herself to work a full year, still in intense pain the entire time. She went home each day in tears and crawled into bed immediately until it was time to wake up. Surgery may have been necessary to stop the progression of symptoms, but the recovery process was anything but straightforward, as you will later learn.

HARD WORK ≠ SOLUTION

In December of 2012, I visited an indoor trampoline park with some friends. I went to buy a bottle of water but was instead handed a cup of tap water. A few days later, I was laying on the couch when I became lightheaded and nauseous. As I battled intense stomach pain, I noticed my glucose levels were dropping. I waited in misery until I had a black bowel movement, which meant there was internal bleeding. My mom rushed me to the emergency room.

I was sent to the front of the line at the emergency room because of my immune deficiency, and I drank apple juice to raise my glucose levels while the nurse injected an IV for fluids.

The doctor ordered the typical blood tests, CT scan, ultrasound, and X-ray. Even after the intense invasive testing, the medical staff still had no idea what was wrong with me, so I was admitted to the hospital and spent the night on the surgical floor. A doctor came in to tell me that I needed to have my appendix removed in the morning. The pain was becoming sharp and unbearable, so I took Zofran to calm my stomach and painkillers to calm me down. The doctor was telling me all of this while my hospital roommate screamed in pain from his post–spinal surgery blood transfusion. As a seventeen-year-old, I was shocked and disoriented.

Shortly after, I was told I had appendicitis. Twenty minutes later, the doctor came back to tell me the problem was with my gallbladder, and I still needed surgery. For the third time, the doctor came back to tell me I did not need surgery, but I needed to have an endoscopy. I was diagnosed with Helicobacter pylori (H. pylori), a bacteria in the digestive tract that can cause a series of digestive issues, ulcers, and even stomach cancer. Roughly two-thirds of the world catch H. pylori, but the majority of people have no symptoms.[35] H. pylori can be transmitted from food, water, or utensils and is very common in communities that lack clean water.

I would never know for certain, but I believe the tap water at the trampoline park was the culprit, since I never drink tap water. I spent four days in the hospital then two weeks at home, missing a period of school before winter break. I was on three different antibiotics and had no appetite, my glucose was high, and I lost motivation to do anything. Only Slim Jims and sweet bell peppers helped get rid of the terrible taste of the medication. I was miserable.

Thankfully, my health improved after three weeks. I was finishing up my senior year of high school, and in March, I started having similar symptoms. I had another endoscopy and was diagnosed with diabetic gastroparesis, which is caused when the nerves within the muscles of your

---

35   Minesh, Khatri, "What is H. Pylori?" *WebMD*, December 7, 2020.

stomach are damaged. Diabetic gastroparesis is also typical in diabetics with poorly controlled blood glucose levels.[36] Essentially, I had digestion difficulty and frequent heartburn, nausea, and bloating. The condition has no cure, and the few prescriptions that exist did nothing for me.

Between the two illnesses, I missed five weeks of school, and I received a notice that I might not graduate on time. I was incredibly stressed out and nothing worked. My doctor advised two options: first, an endoscopy every few months to create a hole in my digestive tract, or second, a pacemaker to replicate the way my stomach should work. Both of these options were far from ideal, so I decided to tough it out and deal with my pain.

It took eight years to no longer focus on overcoming and think about the Becoming Mindset. The journey was difficult and made me want to give up countless times but was all worth it. While I may never "overcome" diabetes or diabetic gastroparesis, I am able to feel well despite not being healthy. I've found happiness.

---

36 Sathya Krishnasamy, et al., "Diabetic Gastroparesis: Principles and Current Trends in Management," *Diabetes Ther.* (2018): 1-42.

ACTIONS & REFLECTIONS

1. Identify what causes you stress and relief. Knowing what helps or triggers stress will help you improve your mental health.

2. Adopt the mindset that you are unique and having a chronic illness is simply a part of who you are. When you believe that disability is a possibility, you are committing to yourself that you are unique and you are going to keep pushing forward despite any circumstance.

3. Humans are meant to evolve through challenges, and the only way to do that is to try new things. Growth is uncomfortable, but it is necessary.

CHAPTER 4

THE BECOMING MINDSET

———

WHY WE NEED THE BECOMING MINDSET

The Becoming Mindset is all about understanding your story to transform hidden pain, suffering, or illness into your true potential.

No more feeling like a burden. No more blaming the world for your problems. The Becoming Mindset empowers you to take control of what *you* have the ability to achieve while trying to positively influence what you cannot. Once you realize the power you have, you will start to take full ownership of your life. Your happiness is up to you.

In 1997, Tiffany Yu was in a car accident that killed her dad, and she walked away with brachial plexus palsy (nerve damage) in her right arm. As an Asian American, she felt that it was taboo to talk about death and disability in her family.

In 2009, Tiffany decided to defy her family and stop suffering in silence. She shared her story publicly for the first time on a panel at Georgetown University.

In 2017, she went to see a trauma therapist in San Francisco after she had been assaulted in 2016. In 2019, she was diagnosed with post-traumatic stress disorder (PTSD). As Tiffany soon learned, "the only way out is through."

It took Tiffany years to share her story and even longer to see a therapist, but this time was a key part of her healing process.

Since seeing her trauma therapist, Tiffany has stopped experiencing emotional triggers for her PTSD. Her mindset has shifted away from talking about a story of disability and grief to living with it in a healthy way. As part of her identity, PTSD is something she carries with her daily, but she also sees her healing journey as part of her own post-traumatic growth. Knowing that the disability-lived experience is powerful, Tiffany founded an organization called Diversability, which is on a mission to amplify disabled voices.

When I talk with Tiffany, I deeply relate to her because we both endured years of struggle. We felt lost and uncertain about how to fix our health. Even now, as the author of *The Becoming Mindset*, you might feel like I have my shit together. Sometimes I do, but the journey to push forward is a daily battle, and I am still learning how to be in equilibrium without getting stuck in highs or lows for too long.

It takes time to feel well, and the lessons and personal journeys throughout this book are to help you learn from the countless mistakes we have made. The seven principles of the Becoming Mindset will help you to positively change the way you think about your illness. What worked for us might not work for you, but I hope it will help you start your own journey to build strategies and mental fortitude to better manage your health.

MY FAMILY HISTORY DOES NOT HAVE TO BE MY FUTURE

I lost one grandma to dementia and the other to an aneurysm. I lost my grandfather to lymphoma, and his second wife had a stroke. My cousin overdosed, and my uncle drowned to death. My parents each have two different health problems, and I am a type 1 diabetic with gastroparesis.

Some of these health issues might involve our genetics and environment, but after years of research, I feel confident I know what either caused or accelerated these chronic issues: our lifestyle.

Looking at my current family, who learned from their family, I have noticed that we are constantly stressed. Our meals are large and lack nutrition. We barely exercise, and our health is never our priority—even when we claim it is.

After twenty years of being alive, I reached my breaking point. I visited a ridiculous number of doctors and at one point, took twelve prescriptions for my diabetes, sleep, stomach, and allergies. I was mentally exhausted and frustrated. I needed to break the cycle of my family's history.

The first step to changing my environment was leaving my most familiar one. I was a first-generation college student, and I was given a chance to live in San Francisco to work on my start-up for a summer. This was my first time flying and living alone, made harder by the fact that I knew no one. To add to the discomfort, I could only afford to live in a "hacker house," which meant I slept on a bunk bed in a four-story house with twenty other start-up employees. It was a questionable lifestyle whether you have a chronic illness or not, but I was chasing my dreams.

The day before I left for San Francisco, I visited my grandmother, Betty, who was basically a second mother to me. She was an incredible human being, our bus stop was at her house, and we loved spending time together. When I saw her this time, she was in the ICU at Massachusetts General Hospital after having surgery for her aneurysm. She was tired and disoriented and connected to multiple machines but still smiling. I kissed her goodbye before heading off to Logan Airport.

The next morning my dad called, which typically only happens when there is bad news. Despite doctors saying my grandma was recovering, she had died. I was heartbroken and alone. I wanted to fly home, but my parents told me to stay. It was tough to deal with mentally, but the start-up program kept my mind busy. I called my mom daily to make sure she was okay.

As I started to acclimate to San Francisco, one thing became very clear to me: Everyone knew way too much about health and prioritized health. When I had doctor's appointments, the conversations were like night and day compared to conversations in Rhode Island. For my back pain, doctors in

Rhode Island were quick to recommend surgery, whereas California doctors wanted me to correct my breathing with meditation and yoga before trying prescriptions or surgery. I learned about preventative medicine and how food fuels your body. I always thought I knew a great deal about how to take care of my body, but, damn, I was a rookie. It was time to stop talking and acting like I knew everything and continue learning so I could take action. This might be a West Coast mentality, but I wish it was everywhere.

TAKING WELL-BEING TO THE NEXT LEVEL

It was Sunday, February 4, 2018, in San Francisco, and I was watching Tom Brady and the New England Patriots in the Super Bowl. A group of friends from New England got together. Everything was going great. I enjoyed a beer and some guacamole, and it was game time. Unlike most millennials, I never eat avocado, but I decided to be adventurous.

The halftime show ended, and I was in the bathroom vomiting. Everyone was intently watching the game, so my three visits went unnoticed. I did not want attention, so I kept it to myself.

After the game, my roommate Kyle and I ordered a car back home. It was a quiet ride, and when we got out of the car, to his surprise, I told him what happened. If my condition worsened, I asked if he was willing to take me to the hospital. When we got home, I was still sick, and my glucose was 84 mg/dL and dropping. Since I could not hold down food, the only option was to walk four blocks to the hospital.

On our walk, I asked Kyle to distract me from my misery. I have no idea what story he told, but thankfully I was quickly admitted to the emergency room. I drank apple juice to raise my glucose level, and when the nurse was inserting my IV, he struggled to find the vein. I became nauseous and casually asked, "What is the protocol for throwing up?" He told me to look to my right, and I told Kyle to look away. I felt awful.

It is always difficult to be calm in the emergency room because you are managing your own pain while another patient might be yelling about their potential heart attack or is delusional due to an overdose. The best medicine was to focus on my breathing and nothing else.

Eventually, I was admitted for the night until I could hold food down. My mom used to always be by my side, but this time, I shared a hospital room with a seventy-year-old man who was recovering from surgery. Throughout the night, I was woken up to test my blood glucose level. Around 3:00 a.m., one nurse casually talked to me about my diabetes. She asked about how long I have been diabetic, what it is like to live with the disease, and if I ever considered a pancreatic transplant, which I learned my hospital roommate just had. The thought of not being diabetic felt strange; did a cure really exist?

Health care is a massive industry, accounting for $3.6 trillion in 2018.[37] The American Diabetes Association estimated the total economic cost of diagnosed diabetes in 2017 was $327

---

37 "Historical," Centers for Medicare & Medicaid Services, accessed December 10, 2020.

billion.[38] I have always seen a connection to capitalism in health care. Without diabetes, a lot of people would lose their jobs and companies would lose money. I believed a cure was a pipe dream.

Reflecting on the nurse's comments, I realized something: Why do I have to be cured?

I love who I am, and diabetes has made me resilient and kept me mentally strong. If I am not on top of my diabetes, my diabetes wins. Each day requires a fight, so I became a fighter. If I was not diabetic, I am sure I would still have a series of problems in my life, but diabetes has shaped who I am. If you gave me a magical pill to cure me today, I would probably say no.

Of course, I want to avoid worsening my health, but I felt like I was improving. My physical health could be better, but mentally, I was as tough as nails. A cure would be great, but a more realistic option would be learning to accept pain versus blaming it. The problem lies with how we think about pain and how we feel about who we are. Speaking from experience, dealing with a chronic illness can be terrible, but I truly believe if we learn to love ourselves for who we are, our relationship with our chronic illnesses will change for the better.

When I reflected on this hospital visit later, I knew I needed to change. My well-being needed to go to the next level because

---

38   "The Cost of Diabetes," American Diabetes Association, accessed December 17, 2020.

my happiness and health were on the line. I believed that if I changed my mindset and relationship with pain, I would get there. It was time to find out.

PHYSICAL THERAPY, SURGERY & A MINDSET SHIFT

For once, my diabetes was doing well, but my body ached, my sleep was off, and my stomach hurt. I went to see a physical therapist named Joe in San Francisco to resolve my poor hip rotation. I progressed to thirty-five degrees of rotation and then could not go any further. My body was tense, and he noticed poor breathing, so I went to get X-rays of my airway. Sure enough, I had severe nasal passageway obstruction. Barely any air was circulating through my nose, so I went to see an ear, nose, and throat (ENT) doctor. I tried a nasal spray for a few weeks with no improvement, and my physical therapist recommended surgery, as he had had a similar issue corrected. It was a low-risk surgery to correct a deviated septum and reduce my turbinates, and I trusted Joe.

I never had a surgery before, and I was nervous. Nothing else had worked, and it was either surgery or potentially developing more serious breathing issues. I arrived at 8:30 a.m. to be prepped before the surgery, which started at 10:30 a.m. When my name was called and I left my mom and Eiko (who is now my wife), I teared up. I was afraid. The staff comforted me, asking about my life, while a nurse slapped my left wrist to prepare for an IV. Before she inserted the needle, I took a deep breath and yelled "Fuck!" loudly in my head. A 2011 study even found that swearing sparingly can help kill pain—nice to know![39] My glucose was a little high, and it has to be below 200 mg/dL for surgery, so the medical team gave me insulin because, otherwise, I would be at a higher risk for blood clots.

The surgery was scheduled to end at 12:30 p.m. I woke up in a post-surgery recovery room with a tube of oxygen flowing through my nose. It was 3:30 p.m., and I could hear and see but not move. A nurse finally came over and pulled a second IV out of my ankle, which was inserted during the surgery since the anesthesia was not spreading to my body. My blood pressure was high, so I was given fentanyl—the drug that killed my cousin—so I was uncomfortable. My nose was dripping blood, so the nurse took a vacuum tube and sucked blood clots out of my nose which caused relief for fifteen minutes before hurting again. I was a mess and started to question if this was all worth it.

At 1:00 p.m., the doctor told my mom and Eiko that I was recovering and they could enter shortly. They were wrong. At 4:30 p.m., my mom frantically entered the room. I was finally released at 5:30 p.m., and my nose was swollen to the point where I looked like I was knocked out in a boxing match. Can you imagine being left in the dark for almost four hours after your child's surgery? I would definitely be yelling at someone. When I walked out, Eiko was so cute and had a puppy dog face of sadness when she saw me with my nose mask to catch the blood. She was incredibly

---

39   Maria Szalavitz, "Why Swearing Sparingly Can Help Kill Pain," *Time*, November 23, 2011.

supportive—one of her many wonderful qualities that made me want to marry her.

After a few days, I was finally functional, but my nose was swollen for weeks. I kept telling myself to please focus on bettering my health from this point forward. This being my first surgery, like Emily, I thought my problem would be fixed as if a magic wand would fully correct my breathing. That's not how it works. The real work was just beginning because my new mindset was to avoid surgery at all costs. I used the nasal spray and my neti pot and practiced breathing to aid a speedy recovery. I was realistic and did not expect immediate results, and with a routine and two years' time, my breathing feels amazing. I can breathe deeply and play sports again, and I have a new sense of energy.

Our health is a never-ending journey. It's not a game, you can't win, and there is no reset button. Our goal is to limit the number of bad experiences and keep looking forward. There might be invisible barriers that make us question what our role in the world is. If we can change our mindset to understand our value and potentially change outcomes, it will all be worth it.

ACTIONS & REFLECTIONS

1. Stop blaming yourself—no more feeling like a burden, no more blaming the world for you. Take control of what *you* have the ability to control, and try to positively influence what you cannot.

2. A reset button in a video game lets you start over from whatever you choose to do—but in the real world, you must take a moment to reflect on and understand how you got here and determine the path you plan to take forward.

3. Think about what path you are taking to feeling well. Is it the easy or hard route? Should you try something different? Who else can you talk to or learn from to make decisions for your health?

PART II

THE SEVEN PRINCIPLES OF THE BECOMING MINDSET

Over twenty years of mistakes, experiments, research, and conversations, I defined seven principles that I believe will lead to a better life for those who are in chronic pain or chronically ill. The following seven chapters will highlight each principle in depth.

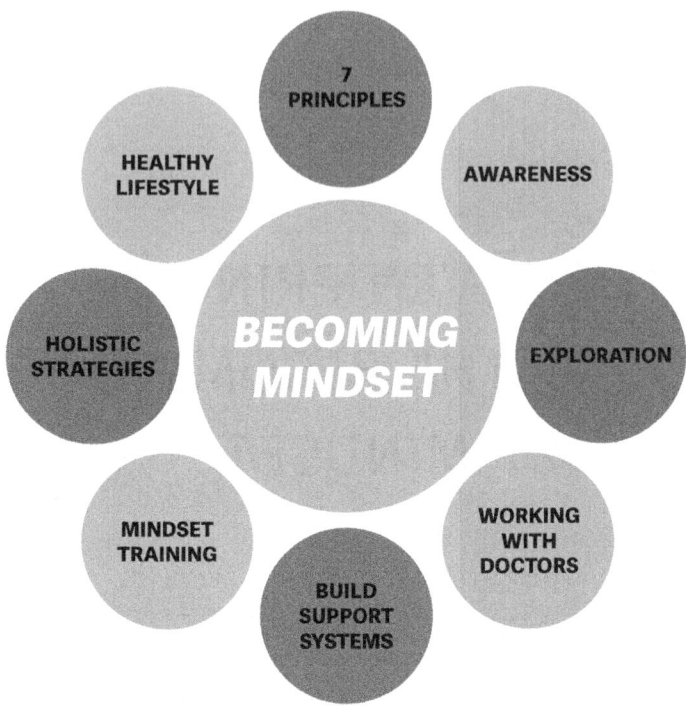

PRINCIPLE ONE: AWARENESS

Awareness is studying what makes you feel well and sick. This includes learning what triggers and heals pain and what helps you embrace your suffering. Pain is a reminder that we are human and alive; when we accept it, we become aware of our bodies' needs, regaining control of our lives. If we listen to what our body craves and dislikes, we can start to make positive changes based on biofeedback.

PRINCIPLE TWO: EXPLORATION

Exploration can include research and conversations with industry experts to look at where your health is now and where you want it to be. Whether it is cancer, diabetes, Crohn's, or chronic back pain, you will find that different treatments work for different conditions as well as different bodies. Knowing that our illness will always be with us, we can begin to comprehend our pain so that we do not feel a loss of control.

PRINCIPLE THREE: WORKING WITH DOCTORS

Doctors' decisions impact our lives in very real ways. They present different options to you, you think about what you want to do, and then you make a decision. Yet, we tend to accept doctors' prescriptions as absolute truths. Your doctor is your health advisor, not your final decision maker. You should be able to work as a team. This approach requires more effort, research, and questions on your part, but it is your body. You need to be in charge of the decisions being made.

PRINCIPLE FOUR: BUILD SUPPORT SYSTEMS

Pain is lonely, and loneliness is a global pandemic. I empathize with what you are going through. What helped me with my own emotional challenges was knowing that there were people around the world going through similar situations. Hearing from them helped me feel less alone. Sharing my story allowed me to learn more about the people around me, support my community, and create new friendships. The internet has allowed us to connect globally, and even though our families love us, we need someone to relate to our pain because it is hard to know what someone is going through if you have not experienced it yourself. Having a solid support system will allow you to feel connected and let you know that you have people who can relate to your pain and care about you. Reaching out is often the hardest step and is nerve-racking, but the risk is worth the reward. If you struggle to find the right community, keep searching, because it exists somewhere.

PRINCIPLE FIVE: MINDSET TRAINING

When you are stressed, your stomach might hurt, your sleep could be off, or you may experience repetitive thoughts. This connection of your body and mind makes mindset training critical. Struggle requires a level of unwavering persistence, believing that you will get better even when you are in immense pain, and turning negative situations into positive learning experiences. Teach yourself that you matter and that you are worthy of loving yourself—and letting others love you back. Mindset training will allow you to find peace, acceptance, and worthiness through your health journey.

PRINCIPLE SIX: HOLISTIC STRATEGIES

While we are accustomed to traditional medicine, checkups, testing, and consultations, we have to explore alternatives to what we are used to, such as holistic medicine. Holistic medicine does not mean going to Tibet for a year and becoming a monk, but it does mean that you are responsible for long-term health care practices that work for you personally. Doctors might prescribe a painkiller or injection, but those are short-term fixes that will likely lead to surgery. What about meditation to relieve stress, yoga to decrease inflammation, or the right diet to help heal your body? What about acupuncture for pain or sleep routines for balance energy? Pairing a doctor's expertise with alternative medicines helps you design your own version of success.

PRINCIPLE SEVEN: HEALTHY LIFESTYLE

What are you eating on a daily basis? How is your environment at home, at work, or within your friend group? Are you exercising regularly? Your lifestyle plays a big role in how your pain is managed. Take a hard look at your day-to-day life, and analyze what you think is working. Make a few changes, see how you feel, and be willing to learn about yourself. It takes patience, time, and experimentation, but once you create the lifestyle that works for you, damn, do you feel good!

CHAPTER 5

AWARENESS

———

EMBRACE YOUR SUFFERING

Once you are aware of your pain, you can leverage it as motivation to work harder.

Going into my freshman year of high school, I joined a five-day tryout for the varsity soccer team. Due to my knee pain over the summer, I was able to avoid running timed miles but still had to attend four hours of daily sessions in the sweltering August heat.

On the fourth day, I went up against the fastest senior in a one-on-one challenge. We got into push-up positions at separate ends of a rectangle, raced to the soccer ball in the middle, and then had to zoom past the other player to get the ball. I won the ball, put it through his legs, and came out successful.

But was winning worth what happened next?

As I took a breath, I could feel that my knee was on fire. I told the captain, who recommended to tell the coach so I could sit out. My pride forced me to keep pushing myself, so I could start on varsity, despite my body telling me to please stop. I remained at the tryout for another two hours and played through the pain, which was the wrong move.

That evening, I could barely walk and went to the doctor. I had an X-ray and ended up in a full leg brace. I had Osgood–Schlatter disease, which inflamed my knee and gave me a painful bump right below my left kneecap.[40] It took four months for my leg brace to come off, and once it did, I developed the same symptoms in my right knee. I wish I had not sacrificed health for pride because if I had acted sooner, my knees might be healed today.

So, beginning at age fifteen, my knees were in constant pain. I was tested for rheumatoid arthritis while working to keep inflammation down. I worked hard to avoid painful cortisone shots to drain the fluid in the bump. I started exploring surgical options. Throughout this process, I did not stop thinking about being on the field with my team, but I made the hard decision to walk away from sports.

It was time to embrace my suffering, turn my pain into power, and put my energy into something else: healing myself.

No one in my entire family history graduated from a four-year college, so I invested more time into my grades. I enrolled

---

40   "Osgood–Schlatter Disease," American Academy of Orthopedic Surgeons, accessed November 21, 2020

in college-level classes, set my sights on college, and became obsessed with learning outside of the classroom. I became (and still am) a straight up nerd, as I started buying coins from around the world, studying World War II, watching documentaries about nature, and collecting rare LEGO sets. Sports were a big part of my identity, but I had to pivot in order to progress.

As I reflected on this time later in my life, I realized that I love sports, but I was too small to ever play professionally. I could have remained stubborn about keeping this a part of my life, but because of a series of injuries, I came to see my health as my wealth. I shifted my energy into new hobbies and passions, opening doors where others had been shut.

ACCEPTING MORTALITY WILL MAKE YOU HAPPIER

One Saturday morning, when I was a junior in college, I woke up to two missed calls: one from my dad and one from my uncle Dave. I called my dad, and he told me that my grandfather was diagnosed with late-stage lymphoma with only a couple of days to live. I was heartbroken because this news came out of nowhere. Before I could go home, I received a call that he was rushed into surgery, and if it was successful, my grandfather (Big Al) might live a couple of months.

Big Al was a hard-nosed Italian. The first time I saw him after he left the hospital, he looked me dead in the eyes and said, "If I die, I die." I was shocked to hear those words, but he was in his eighties, happy with the life he lived and accepting of his suffering. He wanted no more surgeries but agreed to chemotherapy, wanting to be home versus in the hospital.

A survey of American fears found that 20.3 percent of Americans are "afraid" or "very afraid" of dying.[41] If I told you that you had days to live, you would likely become anxious about how you would spend the remainder of your life. So why do we wait to truly live until we know death is on the horizon? I loved my grandfather's attitude because he accepted the suffering, medication, and therapy to enhance the remainder of his life, but mentally, he did not care when he died.

My brother, Uncle Dave, and I visited Big Al. As usual, he was cooking shrimp wrapped in prosciutto, scallops wrapped in bacon, and clams. We were casually chatting while Big Al cooked, and then we noticed that his pants fell around his ankles, and he had no idea. The four of us were crying laughing. I love this memory because, despite a shitty situation, he still found ways to laugh and smile. Big Al wanted to keep living his life, and that is exactly what he did.

Big Al ended up living for fifteen more months. What a badass. His mindset of acceptance decreased his anxiety and stress, extending his life longer than any doctor predicted. If you have cancer and are reading this, you are probably going back and forth to doctors, feeling stressed out, and wondering when it will all be over.[42] One study through the National Institutes of Health found that "various psychosocial interventions in cancer care such as psychoeducation, rational emotive behavioral therapy,

---

41 "America's Top Fears 2017," Chapman University, accessed December 1, 2020

42 "Cancer Survival Rates," Nuffield Trust & The Health Foundation, accessed December 13, 2020.

social support therapy, cognitive behavioral therapy (CBT), and relaxation therapy (guided imagery) are shown to have brought down the level of pain, insomnia, fatigue, loss of appetite, nausea, stress, anxiety, and depression."[43] Decreasing anxiety and stress are some of the best medications you can use.

Even if embracing your suffering does not cure you, it can still calm your brain. Aside from easing your mental health journey, your mindset can alleviate anxiety and stress which weaken your immune system. When you are fighting invisible cancer, your immune system needs all of the strength it can get; so, accepting mortality in your future may allow you to focus on the present life you live.

TAKING ACTION IN AN EMERGENCY
A key part of having a chronic illness is knowing how to act when an emergency occurs.

Jacqueline Claire Calamia was born sixteen weeks prematurely when her mother had a stomach infection and the umbilical cord wrapped around her neck. As a result, Jacqueline was born with cerebral palsy and suffered from seizures as a child. She was seizure-free for fifteen years before losing feeling in the left side of her body. She felt like she was falling and had no idea if she was calling out for help. Then she blacked out.

---

43 Prasad Vijay Barre, et al., "Stress and Quality of Life in Cancer Patients: Medical and Psychological Intervention," *Indian Journal of Psychological Medicine*, (2018): 232-238

Thankfully, Jacqueline's caregiver was home and called 911. She was taken to the hospital and officially diagnosed as epileptic.

Due to her epilepsy, Jacqueline took a daily pill, but after almost two years, a second episode occurred. This time, it was a grand mal seizure, which causes a loss of consciousness and violent muscle contractions.[44] Aware of what seizures feel like, she knew that she had thirty seconds to call for help. Jacqueline's mom carried her to bed and called an ambulance. Jacqueline blacked out on the ambulance ride. Later, she was prescribed Keppra and has since had only four seizures over ten years. But more importantly, Jacqueline began to understand what impacted the severity and frequency of her seizures.

By reflecting on the first two seizures, she learned what the causes were. The first seizure resulted from extreme anxiety and stress. The second was from missing three days in a row of seizure medication. In the following two years, she took the medication daily and deterred the randomness of her seizures.

Awareness is an understanding of what foods, environments, or medications can alleviate or worsen your pain. On a daily basis, Jacqueline has "mental spoons," which she defines as bite-size practices that gauge her capacity and help her to avoid feeling overwhelmed. For example, as a writer, she edits copy and conducts calls with fellow authors. She takes breaks

---

44 "Grand Mal Seizure," Mayo Clinic, accessed November 6, 2020.

and spaces out her work, knowing her limits and honoring her boundaries.

Despite having cerebral palsy, epilepsy, and other health issues, Jacqueline is proud of who she is. She once told me that "if you gave me a magic pill that would heal me, I would not take it." She views her disability as possibility. Jacqueline has good days and bad days, just like every other human being. Jacqueline focuses on what is in her control, what is not, and how to keep pushing ahead—especially when times are difficult.

EMBRACE SUFFERING EVEN WHEN THINGS AREN'T GOING YOUR WAY

Emily Lemiska ran a 5k race and ended up needing serious spinal surgery. Medications, surgeries, moving back home, and going back to work all did nothing to solve her symptoms. She could not lift anything without excruciating pain and feeling like her spine was being yanked. Her focus became simply getting through each day. She stopped volunteering, exercising, and hanging out with friends. Emily relied on her then-boyfriend Dan and her two roommates to help with everything.

Even before Emily's journey with emergency surgery for her tethered spinal cord, a lot happened. Days before the surgery, two very different events impacted Emily's outlook.

One week before her surgery date, Emily's apartment was robbed, which caused disbelief given her current health. It made it difficult for Emily to feel positive in the face of so much negativity.

A few days later, amidst the uncertainty, Dan did something most people dream of: He proposed. Rather than think about what their future might be, which was likely full of doctor's appointments and the need for extra help and care, Dan loved Emily for who she was, and that was truly beautiful. Throughout the first year of symptoms and surgery, Dan referred to Emily as his "brave little toaster," referencing the 1987 Disney movie about an animated toaster who faces many obstacles.

These two events marked the beginning of Emily's journey. She became aware of what her new life might look like, and she wanted to keep fighting until she felt better. It was hard to embrace her suffering, but as you will soon learn, Emily was as tough as nails. She was an expert in using trial and error, creating new plans, and finding ways to smile through what was a long and frustrating process.

Even when things are not going your way, there can still be positives in the negatives. Only focusing on the negatives will keep you in a dark place mentally. On the flip side, positive thinking will help you feel more balanced, even if you are not healthy.

ACTIONS & REFLECTIONS

1. Ask yourself two questions: What am I doing that is working, and what am I doing that is slowing myself down? Make a list, and when one of the items you listed happens in your life, reflect on what you should do—pause, stop, go, whatever you believe is the best path forward.

2. Accept that suffering makes you human. Everyone suffers in some way. Once you accept suffering, you decrease anxiety and stress, which increases your immune health and overall wellness.

3. Control what you can control. Chronic illnesses suck, and there are things you can control. For me, I control what I eat and when. I cannot control the fact that I need to take insulin, but I can influence the dosage and take less insulin by taking care of myself.

CHAPTER 6

EXPLORE YOUR OPTIONS

———

If there is no cure, you have to learn to manage your pain.

As a gamer, I wish life had a reset button. I could press "X," go back in time, generate health, and start over. In life, enhancing your health and well-being requires commitment, experimentation, and reflection to find what works for *you*. Rome was not built in a day, and progress demands patience.

IT'S YOUR BODY AND YOUR DECISION

Most people believe the stereotype that doctors are authoritative figures. However, doctors are not the final decision maker. You are. In season 1, episode 10 of *Curb Your Enthusiasm*, Larry David injures his knee and sees an orthopedist who recommends surgery.[45] He respects the doctor but wants

---

45 "The Spite Store," *Curb Your Enthusiasm*, directed by Jeff Schaffer, written by Larry David, HBO, March 22, 2020.

a second opinion. The second doctor recommends physical therapy and after a few weeks, David heals. He stuck up for himself which can be uncomfortable, but it ultimately led to healing and not undergoing surgery.

For the first sixteen years as a diabetic, I used a syringe and vial to inject insulin. Every day I carried around a frozen ice pack and had to ensure dangerous air bubbles did not get into my syringes. Mentally, I felt like something was wrong with me because syringes always reminded me of being in a hospital bed. As technology improved, I became more open-minded and upgraded to an insulin pen that was stored in my pocket and did not require ice. But I still refused to get an insulin pump because wearing two devices was a constant reminder of being diabetic.

In my third year at Babson College, I was searching for ways to not be in class because I was often sick and needed rest. I ended up writing a fifty-page research paper on glucose monitoring factors, never had to go to class, and received four credits. It turned into a self-study around my blood glucose level, diet, and insulin dosages. I found that my average glucose levels were good, but the standard deviation was too erratic. I needed to change. It was time to stop being stubborn and get a continuous glucose monitor (CGM).

I decided to give the Dexcom CGM a try, and a representative walked me through how to insert the sensor over Skype. Dexcom worked for two weeks, sent readings to my phone every five minutes, and sent alerts when I was trending up or down. Four years later, with numerous lifestyle changes too, my ninety-day average is below 125 mg/dL, which means

I am borderline diabetic. A good benchmark for a diabetic is between 70 mg/dL and 125 mg/dL. My body still struggles with insulin production, but my balanced glucose levels mean fewer issues with my stomach, mind, and energy. My life is literally in my hands, and the last thing I want to do is lessen my quality of life because I was too stubborn to make the right changes.

Looking back, my endocrinologist always recommended an insulin pump during every visit. It always sounded like a sales pitch because my diabetes was under control and I was doing a great job, but do I needed to explore better treatment options? No. At my last appointment, my doctor requested I meet with an insulin pump specialist. I said no, but he awkwardly led me to her office. The medical team gave the initial pitch, I kindly stated I was not interested and did not want to waste her time. I left.

STEP BACK & REASSESS YOUR PLAN

If things are not going your way, take a step back, reassess your plan, and strategize the best path forward.

Sometimes the best solutions to our problems are to swallow our pride, be less stubborn, and do what is best for our health, especially when you are taking the path less traveled. In Emily Lemiska's case, when she recovered at home after her first surgery, she tried countless methods to make progress. She was not sure how long the process would take, and she desperately needed to feel functional. She got to a breaking point, and it was time to change. She started to accept her pain and was determined to heal.

Freelance work occupied her mind and gave her an income, but she wanted to find solutions to her pain. She tried injections, physical therapy, and prescriptions, but nothing worked. After months of exploration, Emily found that a mixture of acupuncture, massage physical therapy, and yoga gave her relief. Since these were not covered by insurance, paying $150 per acupuncture appointment was not sustainable. If you want a short-term fix, like painkillers, your insurance will cover it. If you need a long-term solution, like acupuncture or dry needling, your life savings might be at stake.

Emily knew what worked, so she got creative: regular physical therapy through insurance, meditation, and yoga via guided YouTube Videos, free massages in exchange for helping a masseuse set up their website, and acupuncture every few weeks made possible by finding a clinic that offered more affordable group appointments. She still took medication but at low doses. If your health insurance tells you no, pivot and do the best you can for your health given the resources you have. Beyond physical strategies, learning what types of activities worsened her pain was extremely helpful for Emily. Some activities, like lifting heavy objects, she learned to avoid entirely. Others, she found workarounds for, like using dictation software when her shoulders were too sore for typing. She also learned to pace herself, allocating periods of rest before and after errands or social events.

While pacing yourself might be an unglamorous strategy, it is important in pain management. Emily was fortunate enough to recover from surgery with her family for six months. Time with loved ones was key to recovery because loneliness can consume you. In January 2020, Cigna released a study that found that 61 percent of people felt lonely, and 25 percent felt their mental health was fair or poor.[46] Furthermore, in 2018 the CDC found that one in five Americans will experience a mental illness in a given year.[47]

Emily told me, "Things were so horrible, and I really don't know what I would have done without people like that who let people come live with them for free." No matter who you are or where you are in your life, someone cares about you. If it is not family or people we thought to be close friends, there are thousands of support groups locally and online who are experiencing similar pain. You are never alone.

Even being surrounded by a supportive husband, friends, and family, Emily's level of pain and grief over the loss of her old life, especially her career, made her feel very isolated. And at points, she had dark thoughts of taking her own life, but her mindset kept her alive. Emily always had the sense that anything was better than nothing, and any amount of life she could enjoy was better than nothing. Emily focused on what she enjoyed: writing, cooking, and going outside. Emily came to the realization that things could have been much worse, and she needed to appreciate what she had.

Despite years of trying different options for pain care and feeling grateful for what she had, Emily felt like maybe there is not a cure-all from a pain-care perspective. The pain persisted, and it was time for Emily to create her own care plan

---

46 "Loneliness is at Epidemic Levels in America," Cigna, accessed November 11, 2020.

47 "Learn About Mental Health," Centers for Disease Control and Prevention, accessed November 11, 2020.

and figure out what the best strategy was to take care of her body, which was unique to her.

CHRONIC ILLNESSES CAN IMPACT ANYONE—EVEN THE MOTHER OF DRAGONS

You might believe your favorite celebrity is superhuman, but they are like you and me. They have the same hours in a day, eat and drink to stay alive, and are not immune from chronic illness or pain. Selena Gomez has lupus, Nick Jonas has type 1 diabetes, and Emilia Clarke has suffered from multiple brain aneurysms.

For people with status, life is constantly under scrutiny, which makes it difficult to be vulnerable. It took Emilia Clarke eight years to write her story, "A Battle for My Life," in *The New Yorker*.[48] I was proud of Emilia for her transparency, strength, and courage in showing the unedited version of herself.

But Emilia's story did not end there. As she was filming one of the most talked-about TV shows in history, things started to go wrong.

Emilia was twenty-four years old and had just finished filming the first season of *Game of Thrones* when she became violently ill and fatigued and had a major headache. Her brain was starting to fail, and she was rushed to the emergency room. An MRI diagnosed Emilia with a subarachnoid hemorrhage (SAH), which was a life-threatening stroke.

48　Emilia Clarke, "A Battle for My Life," *The New Yorker*, March 21, 2019.

As Emilia shared, "I later learned, about a third of SAH patients die immediately or soon thereafter. For the patients who do survive, urgent treatment is required to seal off the aneurysm, as there is a very high risk of a second, often fatal bleed. If I was to live and avoid terrible deficits, I would have to have urgent surgery. And, even then, there were no guarantees."

Emilia "had no time for brain surgery" because her priority was acting, not her health. Without surgery, death was all but guaranteed. Surgery was the only option, lasted three hours, and was minimally invasive. However, I still cringed when I read, "Using a technique called endovascular coiling, the surgeon introduced a wire into one of the femoral arteries, in the groin; the wire made its way north, around the heart, and to the brain, where they sealed off the aneurysm." Ouch.

Emilia woke up and was in unbearable pain. Her vision was impaired, a tube was down her throat, and she remained in the ICU for four days. A week later, a nurse asked her name, and she drew a blank. They sent her back to the ICU, but this time she was more cognizant. She acknowledged how lucky she was because others in the ICU did not make it out. It was a reminder that things could be worse and being sick still means you are alive and get to experience the beauty of the world.

Emilia went through weeks of recovery and was finally feeling functional. She struggled while she filmed season two of *Game of Thrones*, but made it through. After season three, she was ambitious and joined a Broadway play. She overdid it. A routine brain scan showed a growth double the size of the first surgery. Another endovascular coiling was done, but the procedure failed. Without a brain operation, she would die. She lived, and the recovery was full of anxiety, pain, panic attacks, and a loss of hope.

You would never know any of this by watching *Game of Thrones*. Even in her interviews, Emilia is a jokester, kind soul, and the type of person who can find a way to make watching paint dry fun. It reminded me that no matter how happy someone is, or how often they smile, you can never truly tell how much they have been through.

Enduring these struggles, Emilia decided to do more than just be a survivor. She started SameYou, which "aims to provide treatment for people recovering from brain injuries and strokes." I did not speak to Emilia directly, but a member of SameYou told me that "in general, Emilia's a very positive and strong-minded person, which is important to get you through the hard times, as the road to recovery can be a very tough and long one in some cases—not only physically but also emotionally. She also had a lot of support from her family and nurse during this time which is also very important as patients can easily feel very lonely and isolated after this traumatic experience in their lives." Pain is not linear. There will be setbacks, detours, and unexpected solutions.

ACTIONS & REFLECTIONS

1. For seven days, record what you eat, when you sleep, your activity, and how each made you feel. Study the results, and understand what worked and what did not.

2. Be comfortable with trial and error. A treatment that works for you works very differently for other patients and vice versa. Explore your options, and do not listen to simply one person. Do your research.

3. Think about one or two transformative moments that impacted your life—for example, getting your first job, becoming a parent, or a hospitalization. How did this moment make you feel, and do you like or dislike that it is a part of your story?

CHAPTER 7

WORKING WITH DOCTORS

———

DOCTORS ARE EXPERTS, BUT EXPERTS DON'T KNOW EVERYTHING

Have you ever had a doctor tell you that all of your pain was in your head? I experienced these words countless times and became frustrated. The other patients seemed crazy, but we went to the doctor because we needed help. Looking healthy and feeling well are two completely different things. This begged the question: Should we believe everything a doctor says?

In the United States, the average time to diagnose a patient with a rare disease is 7.6 years, requiring seeing eight different doctors.[49] Along this journey, you might try tests, undergo procedures, change your diet, or take vitamins.

Invisible diseases, like Crohn's and Lyme disease, lead you to believe patients are healthy, but they are fighting an internal battle. Unfortunately, no matter how hard you work, feeling

---

49   "Rare Disease Impact Report," Shire, accessed December 16, 2020.

well is not meritocratic. Effort does not always lead to the results you expect.

When you look at Emily Lemiska's story, she believed every word her doctor said, and it created false hope because she was not getting better. Her doctor meant well but probably was a bit too optimistic. It was impossible to have an answer to every unique problem. As of October 2019, there have been 318,901 clinical studies by medical teams completed since the year 2000.[50] Our problem is not that doctors are not experts but that they must contend with an overwhelming amount of ever-changing—and sometimes conflicting—information based on literature they study and the patients they have examined.

Every patient is unique. This means while a medication that fixed one person's headache, may have caused a severe allergic reaction to someone else. For Emily, she started to take what doctors said with a grain of salt. It was extremely difficult to believe her care plan was the best course of action when the pain kept worsening. Put yourself in Emily's shoes. If you were a patient, would you rather get a sense of optimism that things will get better or the cold hard truth about your situation?

Ideally, you want a mix of both—a doctor who you trust and who has your health in their best interest and supports you. Ask questions and get options, and then a decision can be made. Emily soon realized how important it was to have a

---

50   Matej Mikulic, "Total Number of Registered Clinical Studies Worldwide Since 2000," *Statista*, February 2, 2021

supportive doctor. If a medication or routine was not working, she needed mental reinforcement that it was not her fault and her medical condition was standing in the way. She also needed someone who took her condition seriously, even though she looked fine. What she did not need to hear were the painful six words that are spoken too often: it is all in your head.

Since doctors are experts, they often feel like they have to supply an immediate answer to your question. Saying "I don't know, but let me ask around and get back to you" is far more respectable than giving your best guess. These guesses ultimately impact the patient, and a confident answer does not make you correct. Question everything, even if you believe they are right.

While doctors are indeed experts, experts need help too. Ask your questions, and understand the positive or negative consequences of your decisions. View your doctor as a consultant and utilize their experience and knowledge, but also perform your own research to make the best possible decision for *you*.

WHAT IF YOU DON'T HAVE A RELATIONSHIP WITH YOUR DOCTOR?

Tiffany Yu was surprised when I told her I had decent relationships with my doctors. Tiffany grew up thinking there was an uneven power dynamic with her doctors, assuming that they knew more than her. This leads to white coat syndrome, which is a spike in your blood pressure due to the nervousness of dealing with a doctor and anxiety over a potential diagnosis.[51] This happens, for example, when you are waiting for the doctor to enter the examination room with your test results and you hear them knock on the door. Whitecoats syndrome is real, and it can be intimidating.

When you visit a doctor, the conversation points to you not being well. For Tiffany, her PTSD symptoms were triggered when visiting doctors because they made decisions about her body and health without much input from her.

Tiffany has had her brachial plexus injury for twenty-three years and does not have ongoing relationships with any doctor related to that injury, partly because she had switched jobs and had new insurance plans but mostly because the focus for recovery was on surgery. She tried physical therapy, but she found it to be harmful in ways because her exercises were fixated on the limitations of her disability and rooted in a medical model for disability. She has taken a more holistic view of physical therapy, incorporating a few physical therapy exercises into her wellness practice.

After inconsistent care with doctors, Tiffany decided to try therapy. Being diagnosed with PTSD twenty-two years after the accident allowed her to explore PTSD-specific treatment. After a year of therapy, Tiffany's PTSD was minimal, and her triggers became manageable. It took twenty-two years to see a therapist, but it was well worth it. The average

---

51   Mariana R. Pioli, et al., "White coat syndrome and its variations: differences and clinical impact," *Integrated blood pressure control*, 11, (2018): 73–79.

delay of onset mental illness symptoms and treatment was eleven years.[52]

Without a diagnosis, the cycle would have continued. Therapy is heavily stigmatized, but being able to talk to a licensed professional about your pain can be magical. Trust takes time, and it takes a large amount of courage and vulnerability to see a therapist. You might feel discomfort at first, but growth is uncomfortable.

Tiffany might not have the strongest relationships with her doctors, but she is not afraid to ask for help, which has led her to feel well despite living with a mental health condition.

HOW TO BUILD A RELATIONSHIP WITH YOUR DOCTOR

Growing up, what did you want to do when you were older? I wanted to be a doctor, which was ironic because I gave my doctors such a difficult time when I was younger. As I aged, I realized how important it was for me to build a relationship with my doctor. It took me twenty years to be great at collaborating with doctors, but it was worth the wait. I refused to be the person who visited my doctor, refilled medications, left, and repeated. I wanted to take less medication, feel well, and gain the knowledge to make the necessary changes to feel well.

---

52   Philip S. Wang et al., "Delays in initial treatment contact after first onset of a mental disorder." *Health services research* vol. 39,2 (2004): 393-415.

When visiting doctors, I recommend you come prepared with research, become comfortable saying no, and fully explore your treatment options.

DO THE RESEARCH AND COME PREPARED

When you visit a doctor, how much preparation do you do? Do you scare yourself by looking at WebMD symptoms, or do you dive deeper into research and bring that information to your appointment? Do enough research to be educated, but do not drive yourself crazy over what might be wrong with you. Once you have a diagnosis, like diabetes, your focus shifts to management. For example, my doctor and I often review the last three months of Dexcom glucose monitoring data to find my average and spot trends. This gives insight into my overall diabetes management as well as into whether we need to adjust insulin dosages. If my doctor recommends changing doses, I give it a try. If it does not work, I message my doctor online and recommend I switch dosages. By using data, my doctor's expertise, and my own research, I am able to make the best decision for my body.

BE COMFORTABLE SAYING NO

Saying no can be difficult and is often seen as a negative action because you are turning something down. I disagree.

Standing up for yourself is empowering. When I was eighteen years old my sleep was terrible, and I constantly woke up throughout the night. I performed a sleep study, woke up over ten times, and was diagnosed with chronic insomnia. My doctor prescribed a sleeping pill, trazodone, which led to demonic nightmares. After two days, I stopped. My doctor recommended a stimulant, Adderall extended-release (XR). It made me emotionless—on constant high alert—and while I slept better, mentally, I felt like a zombie. It took eighteen months to schedule an appointment with my sleep doctor, but I needed to get off of this medication. My doctor created a safe plan to get off the medication, and once I stopped, I slept for twelve hours a day for two weeks. Then I was fine. Now when doctors recommend increasing a medication dose, I ask questions and practice saying "no" when it doesn't make sense for me.

EXPLORE TREATMENT OPTIONS

Whether you require surgery or are fixing your allergies, you have to assess each option. In the summer of 2020, I had a painful ingrown nail removed. My options were to see if the nail healed on its own over three weeks, try at-home remedies, or have a quick removal procedure. I asked the doctor about the benefits or risks of each and decided the procedure made the most sense since diabetics are prone to infection.

Another example was when I fell off a hammock and banged my head on cement. The medical team at the urgent care clinic started preparing IV fluids and an injection for the pain. I was confused and told them to walk me through the plan first. It made no sense, so I asked if drinking water and taking ibuprofen would work and they said yes. I chose the latter, and after a few days, I was fine. I wish they had explained my treatment options, but thankfully, I stood up for my body.

In September of 2020, I was sent to the emergency room for fear of my appendix bursting, and I got to talk to the doctor for twenty minutes. He told me that his job is to make the best medical decision for me based on what he knows. He felt that patients may not always like what he has to say, but he can sleep at night knowing he did the best he could. I found this admirable, but it also alludes to the point that doctors are on your side but, ultimately, you are in charge of your life. Doctors care about you, but you have to care about your body the most. The moment you leave their room, they have to help someone else. Regardless of how many patients they see a day, they do not live with the results. You do.

THINK OUTSIDE OF THE BOX

Searching for a solution to my diabetic gastroparesis, which is a digestive condition, took me on a seven-year journey with doctors in Providence, Boston, San Francisco, and New York. My doctors told me that my gastroparesis was mild and that I was fine. I felt horrible. One of the top gastroenterologists in New York City recommend a probiotic to aid digestion, but the pain persisted. It was time to move on.

After seven years, I finally found a doctor willing to think outside of the box. Dr. Rogers at Mount Sinai Hospital had empathy for my frustration and took a step back. Doctors tried different medications without success, so he recommended a powerful medication: changing my diet.

He did what every doctor should do. He asked me about my work and home life, stress, and other external factors that might be causing my gastric issues. We quickly realized how much stress triggered my stomach issues.

The plan was to continue my vegetarian diet but eat more fiber, fruits, and vegetables to aid digestion as well as meditate every morning, take breaks throughout the day, and go for an afternoon walk. With less inflammation, I began feeling far more functional.

Whether it was my physical therapist, Joe, who focused on breathing or Dr. Rogers who offered a different strategy than previous doctors, thinking outside of the box can help you become focused on healing when most options have been explored—especially when you have a chronic illness, which is difficult to treat and has no cure.

This all empowered me to be the biggest advocate for my health. A few years later, in 2018, I fell ill with a stomach bug. When I was in the emergency room at the University of California, San Francisco, the head doctor asked me an important question.

"What do you think we should do?"

For once, a doctor was not telling me what to do but was working with me to find a solution. When I recommended that I spend the night since my glucose was low and I could not hold down food, he smiled. "I love a patient who knows their disease."

I was given a choice, which was new to me. Usually, the doctor prescribes medication, orders a test, and gets defensive when I push back. My exchange with this ER doctor was refreshing. I will keep saying it: You are more in charge of your life than you believe. But first, you must mentally accept that you are.

ACTIONS & REFLECTIONS

1. Next time you go to the doctor, prepare a list of questions based on your research. Push back on their answers to dive deeper into their thinking and your options.
2. For serious procedures, diagnoses, and other important decisions, get a second opinion. You are not disrespecting the doctor, but you are simply gathering more insight to support the decision that you make.
3. If you have been seeing the same doctor without much improvement, find a doctor who thinks outside of the box. Sometimes the solution is as simple as fixing your diet.

CHAPTER 8

MINDSET TRAINING

———

We are our own worst critics.

We doubt what we can achieve. We criticize ourselves. When we receive nine positive comments out of ten, we are fixated on the one negative comment. Growing up, negative thoughts controlled me because I was constantly sick, and school only added to my stress. After recovering from a health issue, I would take extra days off so I could start fresh the following Monday. This constant back and forth created a pattern of exhaustion and isolation.

The biggest positive change happened when I looked at my health from a rational state of mind. For example, if in the emergency room, I waited for the worst diagnosis. Was it cancer, did I need surgery, or was something mysteriously wrong with me? I typically overestimated the reality, which was more like a stomach bug or gas trapped in my intestines. Based on my past catastrophizing, I trained myself to envision the best case, the worst case, and the most likely diagnosis I would receive. In mapping potential outcomes, I was often less surprised when the doctor gave a diagnosis.

Suddenly, the anxiety and stress of waiting decreased, and I was more prepared to get an answer.

This self-directed guidance came through for me in August of 2020. After a video visit with my doctor, I was rushed to the emergency room terrified that my appendix would explode. I paused, took a deep breath, and called my mom, who drove me to the hospital. The nurse offered me painkillers, but I chose to breathe slowly and distract my mind. If surgery had to happen, it would save my life. I continued to focus on my breathing, keeping myself calm and strong.

I ended up being diagnosed with abdominal and intestinal inflammation. Within a few days, I was back to work and functioning.

THE SECRET TO BECOMING MENTALLY STRONG

When everything goes well, our mind feels strong. When things go wrong, anxiety and stress take over. So how do you build resilience to prepare you for the challenging times? According to psychologist Amy Morin, you must reframe three types of unhealthy beliefs.[53]

First, we must address our unhealthy beliefs about **ourselves**. We often say, "Why do these things always happen to me?" We feel sorry for ourselves because we are too focused on the problem. We believe we are the only ones who experience pain. However lonely our pain was or is, we are not alone.

---

53   *TEDxTalks.* "Amy Morin: The Secret of Becoming Mentally Strong.," December 4, 2015, video, 15:02.

You have friends, family, or online communities full of people going through pain similar to what you experience.

Second, we must address our unhealthy beliefs about **others**. We often believe that others have authority, are more qualified, or know more than us. The moment you let others make decisions for you, you lose control. For example, if you feel sick but your boss forces you to work, leave until you feel better. If you receive pushback, recognize that your environment is toxic because your health was not the top priority. You only have one life—make it as awesome as you can.

Third, we must address our unhealthy beliefs about the **world**. We are constantly told that if we work hard, we will succeed, but there is never a guarantee. When you believe that the world owes you something, such as success, your unmet expectations will lead to disappointment.

Amy believed that "mental strength is a lot like physical strength. If you want to be physically strong, you need to go to the gym and lift weights." In practice, if you want to build strength, you have to put in the effort. The same is true for resilience.

The challenge, of course, is knowing how to intentionally shape your beliefs. The easy road is filled with avoidance, internalizing, and sulking. This delays finding a solution. I know how hard it is to stay positive, so every time one negative thought enters your mind, think about three positive things. You are awesome, so stop being so hard on yourself. Do not let the four walls of a box contain you. Break one of those walls down in order to make peace with your mind, gain confidence, and become mentally strong.

LIVING WELL DESPITE YOUR CHRONIC ILLNESS

I have known Paola Cordovez for over four years, and I just found out she has Crohn's disease. I always knew Paola to be extremely ambitious, traveling the world and living her best life.

In high school, Paola had stomach issues, but when they went away, she assumed she was fine. She moved to the United States from Ecuador in 2012, and in early 2013 her stomach hurt daily.

After going to the emergency room, the doctors said it was either colon cancer or Crohn's. Cancer was the worst-case scenario, but Crohn's would never go away. Paola was diagnosed with Crohn's and never told her family because she did not want to feel like a burden. Soon, however, she needed help paying for a medical bill, and her parents supported her. She spent the year going back and forth between doctors and was prescribed Humira, a biweekly injection to help her Crohn's. Injections can be painful, so she always went home and ate a massive chocolate cake as a reward. Paola always tried to fight pain with pleasure and laughter.

A Crohn's diagnosis could cause negative thoughts about health and the future—but not for Paola. In early 2014, she planned a three-month trip around the world. She wanted to feel normal, and her attitude was that as long as she could keep doing the things she loved, she would do them because one day that might stop. She was not going to let Crohn's slow her down. At one point, she mentioned her Crohn's diagnosis on social media but then took her post down because she did not want it to define her. She wanted others to see her as the powerful and strong person she knew she was.

"I'M FINE"

How often do you ask someone "How are you doing?" and hear "I'm fine" without any context? It is a simple answer that allows avoidance of feelings as both people move onto the next topic.

I often gave this response, but now I share exactly how I am doing. Whether I have just left the emergency room, am reviewing edits of this book, or simply need a break from work, others hear what I am really feeling. This transparency means I can be my authentic self, which makes me feel more human. People might be surprised by what I say, and I do my best to be kind, but I express the real me. Every time.

So how do you respond to people who say "I'm fine" when you know they are struggling with mental health challenges like anxiety or depression? My recommendation is to let them know what you have observed. Take a deep breath, calm your voice, and let your friend know that you are concerned and there for them. Do it with empathy, and be a solid listener if they are willing to open up. If they choose to not talk, find ways to show that you care. Go for a walk together, send a text, grab dinner together, or try to bring them happiness. When people around me are diagnosed with depression, I keep finding ways to show them that I care about them. I try to remind them that there is a lot of beauty in the world.

As of January 2020, there are 264,000,000 people battling depression globally.[54] Additionally, treatment is often limited to the privileged; "although there are known, effective treatments for mental disorders, 76 percent and 85 percent of people in low- and middle-income countries receive no treatment."[55] That's if they even get the right diagnosis.

Jake Tyler is a thirty-one-year-old man living in the United Kingdom who decided to stop saying "I'm fine."[56]

"It's easy to say 'I'm fine' and not tackle your problems head-on. Illness overpowers you. It takes the wheel, and it steers you away from everyone and everything you love. Towards a dark tunnel."

When Jake finally saw a doctor, it became clear he suffered from depression and suicidal thoughts. His doctor asked an important question: "Do you actually want to die, or do you just not want to feel like this anymore?" Jake's pain had persisted for so long that his dark thoughts led him to think about ending his life. This doctor wanted him to reroute those thoughts.

---

54 "Depression," World Health Organization, accessed January 2, 2021.

55 Phillip S., et al., "Use of mental health services for anxiety, mood, and substance disorders in 17 countries in the WHO world mental health surveys". *Lancet* 370, 9590, (2007): 841–850.

56 *TEDxTalks*, "Jake Tyler: 'I'm Fine'—Learning to Live with Depression," Feb 13, 2018, video, 16:05.

One day, Jake was walking his dog. He accidentally walked twelve miles, and he found himself noticing the color of his surroundings again and smiling. He felt happy for the first time in a while, and he realized that walking in nature was healing for him. This revelation drove him to map out a trek through Britain and start a YouTube channel to capture his journey.

Jake thought that sharing his story would be the scariest thing he ever did, but it turned out to be the bravest thing he ever did. "Once you talk to more people, you realize they have similar stories and that your story might not be the worst, which you likely think it is. Talking about feelings creates trust and community."

I have experienced this firsthand, where being open about my story made others more comfortable opening up about their own stories. I was at a leadership conference and in small intimate groups, and we were asked to share about key moments in our life. People talked about losing loved ones, being sexually assaulted, and more. It made me want to share my story, so I did, and we instantly became friends due to mutual trust.

Working on your mental health is a journey and is all about moving forward. Like Jake says, if you feel worthless, think about the times you were happy. Replicate those events, and try to preserve them in your mind for later reflection. Remember that at some point, someone you know has most likely experienced mental health issues ranging from anxiety to stress to depression. Whether you realize it or not, we are all on the same team.

ACTIONS & REFLECTIONS

1. Think about the worst case, best case, and likelihood. The likelihood is what is most likely to happen. Thinking through each situation helps you avoid surprises. The worst-case will make you anxious, the best case will make you optimistic, and the likelihood will make you realistic. The combination of the three helps you understand the situation.

2. Mental strength comes from confidence—the confidence to not let the four walls in a box contain you. Push through the walls, and break free from your mind. Stop being your worst critic.

3. It is okay to be negative, but find ways to be positive too. It is all about finding a balance between the two.

CHAPTER 9

SUPPORT SYSTEMS

————

LONELINESS IS A EPIDEMIC

If there is anything COVID-19 has taught us, loneliness is a epidemic, and our mental health is at risk. In 2020, Cigna found that 61 percent of Americans reported feeling lonely.[57] The causes? Likely a lack of social support or meaningful social interactions. It could also be negative feelings about one's personal relationships. Whatever the reason may be, loneliness can lead to poor physical and mental health. The CDC reported that social isolation was associated with an approximately 50 percent increase in risk of dementia and other serious medical conditions.[58]

In 2019, my grandmother died from dementia. She was the sweetest woman I had ever met. Her second husband was bipolar, and once the medication started making him antisocial, their weekly outings at the community center

———

57 "Loneliness is at Epidemic Levels in America," Cigna, accessed January 13, 2021.

58 "Loneliness and Social Isolation Linked to Serious Health Condition," Centers for Disease Control and Prevention, accessed January 13, 2021.

stopped. She was home seven days a week and occasionally went for a walk, and every time I went to visit, their eyes were glued to the TV. Once I started hearing the same conversations five plus times per visit, I knew her mental health was declining because isolation was causing mental deterioration.

We all can benefit from some alone time, but who wants to be lonely? Ironically, we are more digitally connected than ever but more disconnected from each other. We constantly stare at cell phones and use social media but spend less time together. It took me a while to realize how many people in my life felt alone. It is easy to feel hopeless and lost because finding the right community takes time, but when you do, the journey is well worth it.

For example, climbing a 2,500-foot mountain is tough and requires resilience to keep pushing forward. You might complain all the way to the top as I do, but once you see the view, you cannot help but smile. Most of us celebrate the accomplishment but appreciate the journey too. No matter what situation you are in, there are people going through similar situations who crave the same connection. If you take the time to put in the effort, you will find the right community to connect with and learn from. You just have to be willing to share your story, and the first time is always the hardest.

CAN'T FIND A COMMUNITY? START YOUR OWN.

Tiffany Yu was nine years old when her dad lost control of the car and died while she was in the car.[59] Tiffany woke up in a helicopter en route to a children's hospital in Washington, DC, where she would be for the next three weeks. The broken bones in her legs healed after a few months, but her brachial plexus (nerve) injury in her arm will always remain with her. At school, she felt totally excluded. Anyone with a chronic illness or disability will tell you that the worst part of the school day is gym class. You typically get picked last and kids avoid you because they don't really understand what to say or do.

People who interacted with Tiffany were often uncomfortable with her disability and would stare at her arm. She just wanted to be accepted and understood, yet people were afraid to say something because it might be offensive. In her TEDx Talk, "The Power of Exclusion," Tiffany says, "[The media] portray[s] disability as a medical diagnosis, a tragedy, or a charity case, which is very much rooted in pity and how I saw my own story, or as a function of our external social environment and attitudes. But the problem with these mindsets is that they're rooted in assumptions—assumptions that people with disabilities can't achieve and can't dream, and because of that we're not even given the chance to succeed. And we start to believe that for ourselves. We see the disability, and we judge the ability. But the thing is, no one asked me how I wanted to be viewed." It was time to change.

---

59   *TEDxTalks*, "Tiffany Yu: The Power of Exclusion," April 4 2018, video, 10:57.

Twelve years later, when Tiffany was twenty-one years old, she decided to stand up for the one billion people in the world with disabilities.[60] If you want to be connected and feel heard, you need a community. When she was a college student at Georgetown, she grew a community of over four-hundred members. Six years later, Tiffany re-launched Diversability, a social enterprise to celebrate life with a disability through the power of community. The group has thousands of active members in a Facebook community, and Tiffany is now on the Mayor's Disability Council for San Francisco, is the global disability inclusion lead for the World Economic Forum, and is an active leader in the disability space. But it took time, as does every great beginning.

When Tiffany first marched in New York City's inaugural Disability Pride in 2015, she was the sole person representing Diversability. She believed in what she was building because it was something she desperately wanted when she was growing up, and as a result, she found her purpose in life.

Tiffany often gets the question, "What advice would you give to younger people with disabilities who are struggling with their self-esteem, self-worth, or self-confidence?" The answer is always rooted in community, followed by possibility models and mentors. A healthy support system will have the trifecta. In the case of Diversability, no one is forced to post, but many people appreciate reading the conversations within the community. Tiffany recommends Facebook groups because there is a group for everything. Maybe the group you need is not about chronic disease or

---

60   "Disability Inclusion," World Bank Group, accessed January 13, 2021.

disability but rock climbing or yoga; groups exist for all. Even reading comments is an action that means you are not alone.

As you grow up, the number of people you know will often get smaller; therefore, having a community is especially important. People start families, move, and have their own lives, so what do you do? You find community. Tiffany finds communities, builds trust overtime, and then becomes raw and unfiltered. It allows her to be vulnerable and get the help she needs, as well as contribute to the community.

There is likely a community out there for you, so if you see a gap, fill it. Disability is a possibility, not a blocker. Your story matters. Imagine what it is like when you can go through pain together with others? Because diabetes is technically a disability (and chronic illness), I am now officially a part of the Diversability community. Everyone is welcome.

DIGITAL COMMUNITIES & SOCIAL MEDIA
Despite being in marketing, I tend not to enjoy social media. I view social media platforms as distraction tools that aim to build community but make us feel disconnected. Social media sites are focused on users getting "likes" on photos and using data to create revenue through advertising, and this is far more important than creating authentic communities. However, there are benefits of using social media in moderation, such as connecting with your communities or chatting with friends who are not physically located near you, especially if you have a chronic illness or disability that is making you feel disconnected.

My disdain for social media shrank after hearing Madeleine Boyson give a TED Talk about the relationship between chronic illness and social media.[61] Madeleine went to study abroad at Oxford University in 2014 but, after being diagnosed with Lyme disease, had to return back to the United States for extensive antibiotic treatment and IV therapy. There were days when she could not leave her bed and would stay home and sleep the day away. We have all had days like this, but this was happening daily for Madeleine.

Living in the Northeast, I am often paranoid of Lyme because if it is not found early and treated with antibiotics, being functional is difficult. I had a good friend in college named Emily, who suffered from chronic Lyme who had to constantly visit the doctor and have a PICC line through her arm to deliver lifesaving medication to her heart. Despite giving myself six injections a day, seeing her PICC line made me cringe a bit. I thought she was incredibly brave and tough.

Even though Madeleine's family was supportive and cared for her daily, she felt isolated because they could not understand her pain and what she was going through. She wanted empathy and conversation with other people going through Lyme and experiencing the same problems. I always love talking to other diabetics about best practices and experiences, so I totally understand the craving. Madeleine found multiple

---

61   *TEDxTalks*, "Madeleine Boyson: Chronic Illness and Social Media," June 10, 2016, video, 17:28.

communities full of people who were also suffering from Lyme that were relatable and sparked conversations.

The Pew Research Center found that one in three American adults goes online to figure out what medical condition they have, and 77 percent of online health seekers started with a search engine like Google (whereas only 1 percent started with social media sites like Facebook).[62] Why? Google is easy. You search, you get results, you read them, you draw a conclusion, and you go to a doctor. With Facebook groups, you have to find the right one, get approved to join, create an appropriate post, get credible responses, and then draw a conclusion or see a doctor. It takes time, but the Facebook groups are much more helpful. For example, I wanted to have a stronger nutritional understanding, so I joined a few holistic diet groups. People talked about vegetables and seeds I had never heard of, but now I consume chia and flax seeds daily and feel great. If I went to a search engine, I likely would have ended up at a doctor or on more pills.

In Madeleine's case, she started posting about different medications she was taking and recaps from doctor's visits. She felt comfortable with the group so she not only shared the wins but also the struggles, and regardless, people responded with love and support. She even started getting direct messages from people she had never met—people she now considers dear friends. I frequently post about my type 1 diabetes, and I have the same response. Some people tell me I am brave, but I just tell them I am sharing my story and hope it helps

---

62   Susannah Fox, "Health Online 2013." *Pew Research Center.* January 15, 2013

someone. Ultimately, digital communities are support groups, and when you are there for each other, magic happens.

As the French novelist Alphonse Daudet once said, "Pain is always new to the sufferer but loses its originality for those around him."[63] I realized how true this statement was when I started paying attention to the reactions of people when I told them I was not feeling well. I noticed most people gave a half-smile and wanted to move on from the conversation, maybe because they were uncomfortable. Some people truly care about your pain and want to help, but honestly, most people have no idea how to react. This can make someone in pain feel alone despite being in a group setting.

SUPPORT SYSTEMS AS PREVENTATIVE MEDICINE

In 2016, I was an attendee in a global leadership program called Hive, and a speaker named Ashanti Branch was leading a workshop called "Taking off Your Mask." We sat in two circles and were handed a piece of blank paper and colored pencils. We were asked to draw what we thought a mask looks like—an animal, the phantom of the opera, a scary mask, whatever you wanted. On the front, we wrote down the three things we wanted people to see when they interact with us—confidence, happiness, hardworking attitude, and a bunch of positive statements. On the back, we shared three things we would rather not let people see unless they asked and we trusted them—anxiety, stress, depression, loneliness, and the list goes on. We stood up and had a snowball

---

63   Sebastian Smee, "You Might Think You Know Frida Kahlo But You'll Never Understand Her Pain," The Washington Post, February 14, 2019

fight to anonymize each person's mask. As a group, people volunteered to read out what others wrote on the front and then the back. It made us realize we were not alone. In a room full of brilliant leaders from around the world, we were all going through something that was hiding behind our invisible mask.

Ashanti believes that if you have people in your circle who you can speak to about your struggles, you know where to go for help. But if there is a lack of trust, how can anyone connect meaningfully? We all have friends we talk to about sports, the weather, and basic matters in life, but how do we get real with our feelings? It takes time, vulnerability, and a willingness to speak to a group that is willing to not just hear you but truly listen to you. After all, according to Maslow's hierarchy of needs, the order is food, water, and shelter, and then connection.[64] We all crave connection. Starting from the moment babies are born, they rely on their guardians to be comforted and held. We need each other to survive.

In 2004, Ashanti was a teacher and started organizing weekly lunches where young men could talk about what they were going through. It was important that it was a safe space and happened consistently each week at the same time. It was all about connecting, reflecting, and building community. For many of the students, this was the first time they had a room where they could talk about their emotions openly. Ashanti always starts by sharing the traumatic experiences of his childhood so that everyone feels like they can trust him

---

64   Saul McLeod, "Maslow's Hierarchy of Needs," *Simply Psychology*, December 29, 2020

through vulnerability, which typically leads to a willingness to share their story too.

Ashanti ended up starting a community called the Ever Forward Club, which helps young men grow trust and realize their dreams through the community. Ashanti believes there is something incredible inside of you. Maybe something terrible has happened to you, but you are still amazing. Here is what happened to me. Everyone wants to feel amazing, but most of the time people do not. So how do you get to the point where you believe how awesome you really are?

Once, a middle school teacher told Ashanti he was amazing and had potential. At first, he did not believe her, but once he did, he began to act on those beliefs. It changed his life, so he wants these young men to feel inspired and acknowledge that they are amazing and to help them realize their full potential. Maybe today you can too. I can't promise anything, but I can just hope that you will find the part of you that is absolutely amazing.

When someone shares their story, it can also be that they are inviting you to share your story too, if you feel comfortable. In a group setting, you don't have to share your story out loud or even share your name. It is optional. However, when you see other people willing to do it, it can often give you the courage to step outside of your comfort zone. Finding a support system that is both consistent and welcoming is key because it creates a safe space to keep opening up. You will never know the power of sharing your story unless you give it a try.

In life, most people work harder to avoid pain rather than achieve pleasure. The internal debate of "Am I going to try and use my time to avoid pain?" is exhausting. We have defined pleasure as the positive parts of our life, which actually makes life difficult because it puts us in self-preservation mode versus a model of "If I want to do it, I am going to do it." Ultimately, support systems are incredibly powerful tools to help you feel connected and not isolated. Holding in your feelings is harmful to your mental health, and there are other people going through similar situations that really need to hear from you, and vice versa. If you join a community that is not the right fit, feel free to leave. There is no expiration date on finding community. Take the effort to find the right community because it will make a positive impact on your life.

ACTIONS & REFLECTIONS

1. Search online for forums and groups that have a community with people experiencing similar challenges as you. Digital communities contain an abundance of people and stories that can lead to new friendships and inspiration.
2. Tell yourself "my story matters," until you believe it. The world needs to hear what you have to say. You may think people will judge you, but I bet you will be surprised when you receive support and connect with people going through similar experiences.
3. Find someone you trust, and start sharing your feelings. It might be a friend, family member, a new person in your life from a specific community, or a therapist. Bottling up negative thoughts is detrimental to your physical and mental health, and you can take small steps to start expressing how you feel.

CHAPTER 10

TRADITIONAL + HOLISTIC MEDICINE

———

WHY WE STILL NEED TRADITIONAL MEDICINE

The United States health care system is fundamentally broken, but we still need health care. The best way to understand a country's health care progress is through life expectancy. We are living longer, and "since 1900 the global average life expectancy has more than doubled and is now above seventy years old."[65] The United States currently has a life expectancy of seventy-eight years.[66]

People are living longer, healthier lives as modern medicine evolves. Medical advancements such as imaging, tests, and treatments are detecting chronic illnesses earlier. Vaccines against the flu, smallpox, and now COVID-19 and newer, less invasive surgical methods also add to the average life

65 Max Roser et al., "Life Expectancy," *Our World in Data*, October 2019

66 "World Development Indicators," World Bank Group, accessed January 18, 2021.

expectancy. Modern medicine has come a long way, but there is still progress to be made.

Traditional medicine is critical for performing checkups and correcting health issues. Checkups are a strong preventive measure because you might feel fine, but you may need help. Maybe during your physical exam, your doctor realizes how fatigued your eyes look and hears about the frequent headaches you have. Then there is blood work, which we all hate, but it is a strong diagnostic test. These appointments likely feel like a nuisance but are vital for staying healthy.

I am grateful for the doctors who have given me the proper antibiotics to overcome bronchitis, the scientists who provide insulin to keep me alive and enhance my wellness, and the practitioners who support the medical ecosystem, but traditional medicine is not nearly enough. It is expensive, often only solves short-term problems, and is far too focused on reacting to a health issue versus trying to prevent it in the first place.

When looking at my own life, insulin was not created until 1921 by Frederick Banting. Prior to the invention of insulin, "It was exceptional for people with type 1 diabetes to live more than a year or two."[67] We, diabetics, went from living no more than two years to having devices we can wear that inject insulin for us throughout the day—all in one hundred years. Better treatments are a start, but we need cures.

---

67   "First Use of Insulin in Treatment of Diabetes on This Day in 1922," Diabetes UK, accessed January 18, 2021.

HOLISTIC MEDICINE CHANGED MY LIFE

When I first visited San Francisco, every person I talked to felt like a health expert. People took the liberty to research, experiment, and find strategies to enhance their own wellness—without a medical degree and with simply a willingness to live well. Coming from a blue-collar family in the suburbs, I had an entirely different approach to health. These people gave a shit about their well-being.

If you spend all day in construction as a roofer, your knees and lower back are going to hurt at some point. We just had our kitchen remodeled, and all four workers shared that they had back and knee pain. If a doctor tells you that your options are to take a few painkillers, get an injection, or try acupuncture and yoga, what option do you take?

Pills and injections are the easy routes, and while they might provide relief in the short term, their efficacy will wear off. So you raise the dose. Now you are reliant on these treatments, and without them, your pain is unbearable. On the other hand, remedies like acupuncture and yoga are forms of preventative medicine and long-term wellness.

My mom is experiencing back and neck pain now, too. She gets injections and they help, but after a few weeks, the pain comes back and she needs another injection. For months, I asked her to do yoga or go for a walk with me, and she refused. I was persistent and kept trying to figure out what makes her more willing to try something different. I told her I might give acupuncture a try because it worked for me in the past, and through hearing why I wanted to go, she became willing to try. After a month of appointments, she has actually started to feel better. Her open-mindedness to try acupuncture felt like a win, and pain relief was the icing on the cake.

My mom is not alone because over one hundred million Americans have chronic pain per year which results in $600 billion a year in medical treatment spending and lost productivity.[68] In fact, the Institute of Medicine found that "pain is not optimally managed in the United States and that effective treatment of chronic pain will require a coordinated national effort to transform how the public, policymakers, and health care providers view the condition. Pain prevention is best for your long-term well-being, but it requires more work than short-term solutions like a pill or procedure."[69]

If you asked me four years ago to try meditation, yoga, or acupuncture, I would have stared at you with confusion. Acu-who? Medi-what? Yo-how? To me, holistic health is thinking about the whole body and mind—surrounding yourself with the right people, knowing how to get out of situations that trigger stress, becoming financially stable, eating the right food, sleeping, and ultimately, finding what keeps you feeling well. When your mind and body are in sync, you feel great. When they are at odds, such as having too much stress, your stomach will hurt, your sleep will suffer, and small problems feel massive. Everything is connected. So, what does this look like in practice?

---

68   Salynn Boyles, "100 Million Americans Have Chronic Pain." *WebMD*. June 29, 2011

69   Salynn Boyles, "100 Million Americans Have Chronic Pain." *WebMD*. June 29, 2011

TRADITIONAL + HOLISTIC MEDICINE IN PRACTICE (ROUTINE)

One of my favorite athletes, Michael Jordan, once said, "If you're trying to achieve, there will be roadblocks. I've had them; everybody has had them. But obstacles don't have to stop you. If you run into a wall, don't turn around and give up. Figure out how to climb it, go through it, or work around it." Essentially, when your back is against the wall and you feel like you are out of options, you have to fight and push forward. Giving up is easy and typically unrewarding. Pushing forward is difficult, but that is where positive change and growth occur.

In the case of Emily Lemiska, her back was against the wall countless times, and she did not write off any treatment. There was no one solution that worked for her, so caring for herself became a series of trial and error. Despite the costs of acupuncture, Emily found the treatment to be quite effective in dealing with flare-ups. Acupuncture is a fairly low-risk therapy and can trigger a bad muscle spasm from time to time, but when it works, it is really effective at relaxing muscle tension. Even a small decrease in pain brought a smile to Emily's face and gave her a sense of control. For Emily, it was not about making progress but maintaining a baseline and managing flares.

Another strategy that worked for Emily was to focus on mindfulness through meditation and yoga. Meditation and yoga helped Emily breathe and relax, which led to a decrease in stress and tension throughout her body. Her pain was decreasing, her body felt less tense, and her mind was better at coping with the struggles of life with pain. Despite making progress, Emily wanted to keep inching forward and attended a mindfulness retreat at the Kripalu Center for Yoga & Health in Massachusetts.[70] Meditation, yoga, and community events made Emily feel energized.

Meditation might be intimidating, but you do not have to visit a Buddhist temple in Southeast Asia to start. The best place to begin is through a guided meditation on a mobile app like Calm. You can even search via YouTube. The ambient noises and voice of the instructor help you focus better than trying to do so while sitting alone. I have meditated almost two-hundred days in a row, and I cannot tell you how much better my stress levels are. All it takes is ten minutes in the morning or whenever works best for you.

After Emily's retreat, she went home feeling optimistic. Through massage therapy, acupuncture, meditation, yoga, and activity moderation, Emily finally found the combination of strategies that allowed her to manage her pain. For Emily to get to this point took a serious change in her perspective. At first, she searched for a treatment that would completely stop her pain. Once she understood the pain was not going away, she started to accept it, and life got a little easier. The aforementioned strategies kept the pain tolerable, which allowed Emily to be in control. Emily's physical and mental health were growing in strength despite a long journey.

As Emily started to heal, she reflected on her journey to this point. She quickly realized how one of the biggest problems

---

70   "Insight Meditation for Calmness and Clarity," Kripalu Center for Yoga & Health, accessed January 25, 2021.

with pain management is how we stigmatize pain. Due to the stigma in which pain is seen as weakness, people want to figure out ways to ignore their pain, push through it, or hide it. This way of thinking is detrimental because people really need to take care of themselves. How can you open up when you feel ashamed about having pain or a chronic illness? Often, the thought of how someone might react will stop you from talking. You can get stuck in your own head. Try to share your pain, and if they reject you, they are not your true friends, and you might be better off without them.

Emily's pain stabilized, but her mindset was the ultimate factor. In Viktor Frankl's book *A Man's Search for Meaning*, he quotes German philosopher Nietzsche: "If you have a reason to live, you can overcome any obstacles and survive the tremendous amount of pain." Frankl survived three concentration camps during World War II, including Auschwitz, and he experienced a great deal of pain. Pain impacts us all differently, but how we learn to live with and accept our pain will often dictate how much we struggle.

BUILDING A ROUTINE HELPS YOU BE ON TOP OF YOUR HEALTH

One of the best ways for me to test traditional and holistic medicine was through establishing a routine. My schedule has always been erratic, so a routine forced me to test different treatments to understand what worked and what did not.

According to the *European Journal of Social Psychology*, it takes sixty-six days for a new behavior to become automatic, or a routine.[71] Therefore, I set out to track my progress over seventy days (ten weeks). After some reflection, I wanted to have less stress, sleep better, eat well, and decrease gastrointestinal inflammation, and on top of all of this, I thought I could set extra goals. I was overly ambitious.

I realized there were four specific areas I needed to improve:

Mindfulness: meditation, yoga, and a daily walk outside.

Sleep: same bedtime and wake-up time, no tech before bed, and limiting the number of times I wake up through the night.

Nutrition: eat more fiber, fruits, and vegetables, as well as limit alcohol consumption.

Extra Goals: sports activity, strength and conditioning, and intermittent fasting.

The first week of the routine was a flop. Nothing was tracked, and it was overwhelming. These were the right areas to explore, but the approach was wrong. It was time to go back to the drawing board.

The best approach was to simplify my goals and have someone hold me accountable. My wife, Eiko, agreed, and we

---

71 Benjamin Gardner, et al., "Making health habitual: the psychology of 'habit-formation' and general practice." *The British journal of general practice: the journal of the Royal College of General Practitioners, 62,*605, (2012): 664–666.

listed these goals publicly on the fridge. The list was updated throughout the day and was on my mind every time I entered the kitchen.

Another key decision was to add a recommended time to each action. To avoid being too hard on myself, if I missed an action, I could still perform it later, although—in the long term—chronology created consistency and structure. Keeping track of results daily helped me maintain discipline and create an analysis once completed.

Every day, either a "0" or a "1" was placed in each box. The goal was to have a total score of nine each day, which signaled the entire day was successful. A binary system made the most sense to me because being in the middle felt like I was cheating myself. Each week, I tracked daily percentages to understand how I was doing. Otherwise, how could I know how to improve?

Looking at the ten-week average, 86.51 percent, I started fairly strong and gradually declined until week seven. After some reflection, it became clear more effort was needed. Week eight was successful, but then another slump occurred. It was all mental and winning was on my mind. I knew I wanted to finish strong. I was making progress, but completing one week with 100 percent was my goal, so the challenge continued.

Week # (   )

Task	Times	Monday	Tuesday	Wednesday	Thursday	Friday	Saturday	Sunday
Wake Up	8:00 AM	Wake Up	Wake Up	Wake Up	Wake Up	Wake Up	9:00 AM	9:00 AM
Meditation	8:00 AM	Meditation	Meditation	Meditation	Meditation	Meditation	Meditation	Meditation
Yoga	8:15 AM	Yoga	Yoga	Yoga	Yoga	Yoga	Yoga	Yoga
Usual Breakfast	8:45 AM	Raisins, Fiber & Liquid IV	Raisins, Fiber & Liquid IV	Raisins, Fiber & Liquid IV	Raisins, Fiber & Liquid IV	Raisins, Fiber & Liquid IV	Raisins, Fiber & Liquid IV	Raisins, Fiber & Liquid IV
Brendan Lunch	12:30 AM							
Eiko Lunch	12:30 AM							
Brendan Dinner	6:00 PM							
Eiko Dinner	6:00 PM							
Walk	6:30 PM	Walk	Walk	Walk	Walk	Walk	Walk	Walk
Read	11:00 PM	Read	Read	Read	Read	Read	Read	Read
Bed by	12:00 AM	Bed by	Bed by	Bed by	Bed by	1:00 AM	1:00 AM	Bed by

Daily routine tracker

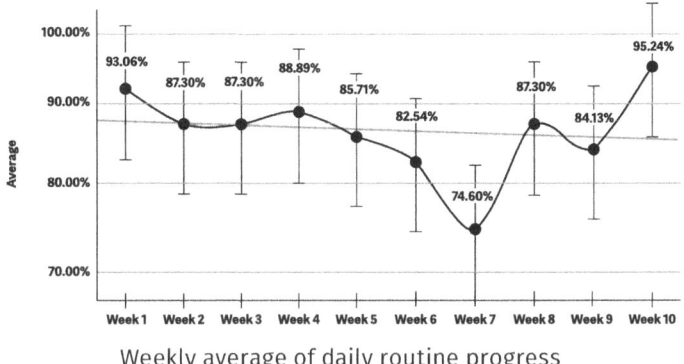

Weekly average of daily routine progress

On a daily basis, weekdays were strong. There was a sense of urgency to get the day started. Data showed that if I woke up on time, that day's routine was 100 percent completed. The exception was when it rained, which resulted in no walk. Waking up at eight in the morning on weekends was unrealistic, so it was changed to nine in the morning. This yielded better results but only started in week eight.

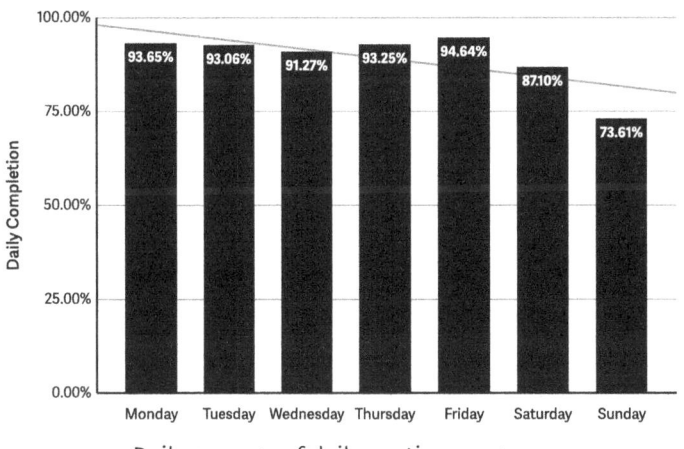

Daily average of daily routine progress

What Did I Learn?

- Tracking your habits helps you understand what works and what does not.
- It is okay to pivot as long as it leads to progress and feeling better.
- Since going vegan and decreasing my stress via this routine, my glucose 90-day glucose level is 123 mg/dL, which is below diabetic.
- Each day is a new day. Learn from your mistakes and start fresh tomorrow.

ACTIONS & REFLECTIONS

1. Research holistic medicine, and see what might work for you. This does not have to be costly. Meditation and yoga can be through guided apps, and nutritionists are in most cities. None of these solutions work in one try, so I recommend being patient and focus on the long-term.
2. Find how to take control of your pain. Whether it is a certain treatment or your lifestyle. You are unique, and finding what works for you is a game of trial and error.
3. Build a routine and stick to it. Routines are hard and take time, but they work. Do you ever think about brushing your teeth or showering anymore? They are natural, and the goals for my life are to embed mindfulness, sleep, and nutrition in my daily routine.

CHAPTER 11

LIFESTYLE

———

Every action has a consequence. We all want to be healthy and feel well, but our actions and lifestyle choices often are the opposite of what would make us thrive.

Growing up, I always wanted to be healthy. But I stopped exercising regularly, took medication more often, and ate and slept poorly. At the time, I felt fine, but I was completely wrong. I did not realize how unhappy I was until I started the journey outlined in this book back in 2018. Testing out lifestyle changes of all sizes slowly has increased my happiness and overall well-being. This journey taught me that human beings struggle to change, but with persistence, trial and error, and willpower, anything was possible.

BLUE ZONES

Blue Zones are located around the world in areas where people live well beyond the national or global life expectancy. The idea came in 2005 with the *National Geographic* magazine cover story "The Secrets of a Long Life," which designated five Blue Zones throughout the world: Okinawa,

Japan; Sardinia, Italy; Nicoya, Costa Rica; Icaria, Greece; and Loma Linda, United States.[72]

Writing in the *Journal of Experimental Gerontology*, Gianni Pes and Michel Poulain expanded existing knowledge around Blue Zones, finding that "Sardinia had the highest concentration of centenarians" in the world.[73] The list of Blue Zones is growing; as of March 2016, the Italian village of Acciaroli reported having three hundred residents over the age of one hundred. So why are people living so long in these Blue Zones? Their lifestyle.

Dr. Alan Maisel, a cardiologist at the University of California, San Diego School of Medicine, led a team to answer the question of what the town of Acciaroli did differently.[74] Dr. Maisel thought good genes and healthy eating would do the trick. He quickly observed two dietary habits: "Everybody ate anchovies, also, every meal, they have the plant rosemary in almost everything they cook." Will you live until one hundred if you add anchovies and rosemary to your daily diet? Maybe, maybe not; but your diet is only one part of the equation.

Dr. Maisel and his team also observed that no one was seen exercising and many of the residents were actually daily smokers and overweight, meaning your diet and winning the gene lottery are game changers. Another incredibly important point is that you will find the community together all

72   "History of Blue Zones," Blue Zones, accessed January 13, 2021.
73   "History of Blue Zones," Blue Zones, accessed January 13, 2021.
74   Felton, Kathleen, "This Italian Village Has 300 People Over 100 Years Old," *Health*, March 13, 2021

afternoon and evening eating and enjoying time with one another. Finally, all of the cities deemed Blue Zones are rather remote, which tends to create a slower pace of life that definitely reduces stress. Having lived in San Francisco and New York City, this totally made sense.

If you want to learn more about what contributes to longevity in Blue Zones, I recommend checking out bluezones.com. The site has recipes, an online community, and different strategies to follow to enhance your life. So, what should you do if you do not live in a Blue Zone? Well, in order to prevent an abundance of health complications, I would focus on three areas that should lower internal inflammation and stress: nutrition, sleep, and community.

NUTRITION

Food is fuel. Water is life. Inflammation is dangerous. The number one question I ask myself before I eat is "Does this reduce or increase inflammation?" Seven years ago, after my gastroparesis diagnosis, my stomach and gastric system were on fire—daily bloating, indigestion, heartburn, no appetite, and frequent nauseous. I felt awful every day. Looking back, the issue was really that I had a shitty diet, ate too much processed food, and barely consumed any fruits or vegetables. The only thing that made me feel better was skipping dinner, which tended to be my largest meal.

The first real positive change happened in June of 2016. I was in San Francisco, and a few of us went out for tacos. I ended up with severe food poisoning that night. Having already had salmonella and food poisoning over five times, I was done with meat. The next day, I quit cold turkey and went vegetarian. I knew very little about what a vegetarian diet was. I even ate fish here and there at the beginning but stopped after a few weeks once I educated myself. I just knew that I needed to feel better.

In theory, I could have easily gone to my gastroenterologist, asked for stronger medication, and not made any lifestyle changes. But it took seven years to even get a recommendation to seriously look at my diet and nutrition. Dr. David Eisenberg, professor of nutrition at Harvard T.H. Chan School of Public Health, states, "Today, most medical schools in the United States teach less than twenty-five hours of nutrition over four years. The fact that less than 20 percent of medical schools have a single required course in nutrition, it's a scandal. It's outrageous. It's obscene."[75] Fewer pills, more nutrition. When I went vegetarian and later vegan, I focused on foods that do not cause inflammation. Within weeks, my body gradually started feeling stronger.

Finding the diet that works for you is about trial and error, then moderation. For example, adding fiber to your diet will aid digestion and bowel movement, and cutting back on red meat will support healthier arteries. You do not have to eat anchovies to live to over one hundred years. Find the healthy foods that work for you. Be adventurous.

Most of what I eat daily now I had never considered trying. I start the day off with raisins, fiber bars, and green tea

---

75 "Doctors Need More Nutrition Education," Harvard T.H. Chan School of Public Health, accessed January 13, 2021.

with the goal of energy aiding digestion. Lunch is usually a smaller meal such as a fruit smoothie, steamed vegetable dumplings, or soba with a mix of vegetables like brussels sprouts, okra, and shishito peppers. For dinner, I eat a fruit smoothie, light pasta, or treat myself to something different. It took me forever to get to this point, so keep trying until you are happy with your choices. Then gradually keep improving.

After going vegan, I experienced less inflammation but still felt gas trapped in my intestines. I had never gone to a chiropractor, and after five sessions of spinal realignment, gas was rarely trapped in my intestines anymore. It was working. My gastric system feels close to healed but not 100 percent, so now I need to focus on strengthening my body so my spine has support. I do this through vinyasa yoga, core strengthening, and proper nutrition. Now that I have a great relationship with food, the next goal is to have a great night's sleep.

SLEEP

I believe that no lifestyle change can negatively or positively impact you more than your sleep. When I sleep well, I feel energized and less stressed, which leads to better blood sugar control and fewer stomach problems. Early on, I learned that sleep was the main indicator of how my day went. I had chronic insomnia for three years and every day was a struggle because I would wake up groggy, yawning, and with no excitement for the day ahead. My mindset was to view each day as an assignment—complete tasks, sleep, and repeat. This was a terrible outlook. Now, when I sleep well, I feel like I am able to conquer the world.

Think about it. Thirty-three percent of your life is spent sleeping. Sleep is important, and how you heal in those eight hours will impact how you feel for the next sixteen hours. Dr. Mark Wu, a sleep doctor and neurologist at Johns Hopkins University School of Medicine, explains that "sleep is a period during which the brain is engaged in a number of activities necessary to live—which are closely linked to the quality of life."[76] Throughout the night, your body is cycling between two types of sleep: rapid eye movement (REM) and non-REM. The two main processes controlling sleep are the circadian rhythm, which is a biological clock based on light, and sleep drive, which Dr. Wu describes as the craving by your body to sleep. Sleep drive is essentially the buildup of exhaustion by your body.

Dr. Harneet Walia, director of sleep medicine and continuous improvement at Miami Cardiac & Vascular Institute, says that "first and foremost, we need to make sleep a priority. We always recommend a good diet and exercise to everyone, but along the same lines, we recommend proper sleep as well." Dr. Walia says that a lack of sleep can impact your awareness, cause daytime sleepiness, impair memory, and decrease your overall quality of life. If you don't address the problem, in the long-term, lack of sleep can lead to serious health problems such as high blood pressure, diabetes, heart attack, heart failure, stroke, depression, and more. Basically, not getting enough sleep, which is essentially a healing mechanism for your body, can have terrible consequences

76   "The Science of Sleep: Understanding What Happens When You Sleep," Johns Hopkins University, accessed January 29, 2021.

for your health and cause a myriad of serious problems. So how do we sleep better?

Dr. Michelle Drerup of the Cleveland Clinic has five incredible tips to enhance your sleep.[77] My sleep has gotten better, but I want to be the sleep expert of my body and plan to apply these tips for my strategies as well:

1. **Look at sleep as medicine.** We all have busy lives, and we likely put sleep at the bottom of our lists, yet it needs to be a top priority. Otherwise, our days will be less effective, and our health will deteriorate overtime.
2. **Have a solid wake-up routine.** Having consistent wake-up times will support your circadian rhythm and help your body understand when it should wake up. It is also helpful to have a bedtime routine to alert your body that it is time for sleep.
3. **No tech an hour before bed.** We love our phones, but the blue light from screens makes it difficult for your eyes to prepare you for sleep. One trick I use on the computer is a program called f.lux, which gets rid of blue light.
4. **If you wake up in the middle of the night, don't look at a clock.** The reason for this is, as Dr. Drerup explains, "You start mental calculations, you think about how long it's been since you've been in bed and what you have to do the next day." As someone who wakes up in the night often, I am guilty of this. I usually put the fan on or put in earplugs to distract myself so I can fall back asleep. It works.

---

77 "Here's What Happens When You Don't Get Enough Sleep," Cleveland Clinic, accessed January 29, 2021.

5. **Make time for downtime.** Dr. Drerup says, "In our society, nowadays, people aren't getting enough sleep. They put sleep so far down on their priority list because there are so many other things to do—family, personal stuff, and work life." Downtime can be as simple as watching Netflix, playing video games, or going for a walk.

I no longer have chronic insomnia, and my sleep has greatly improved, but I still have a long way to go. Tips 1, 3, and 5 have worked well. I get into a routine, but when I fall out of it, it is a struggle. One strategy I use in the morning is to listen to a meditation for 10–15 minutes in bed. Once I finish, I find that the breathing made me more alert and ready to get out of bed. At night, I usually set my alarm for 8:00 a.m. but often change my focus to getting eight hours of sleep if staying up too late. Find what works for you, because sleep is absolutely crucial to your overall wellness.

MENTAL HEALTH THROUGH COMMUNITY

One of the big cultural pitfalls in the United States is how we eat. Roughly 50 percent of Americans eat lunch alone, and 60 percent of professionals eat at their desk.[78] Lunch is not sacred in the United States because we are stressed about deadlines, work, and other responsibilities. When I went to Paris and Berlin for work, I would regularly spend one to two hours eating lunch with teammates. Lunchtime was a chance for us to connect, share stories, strengthen our relationships, and enjoy the atmosphere. In Paris, many of the restaurants

---

78 "The Sad Desk Lunch," Tri-City Medical Center, accessed January 29, 2021.

had outdoor seating that faced the street, almost as a form of entertainment for those who want to connect while being able to take in their environment. Like seventeenth century writer, François de La Rochefoucauld said, "To eat is a necessity, but to eat intelligently is an art."

As an introvert, I definitely appreciate the time to myself and away from people. But too much time alone or too much time with people can make me feel awful. The key is to find a balance. I have a group of friends I play video games online with that I have never met, friends who live across the country that I text and call, and then my core group of friends that I see in person. I prefer to create quality relationships, and I would rather have five great friends than one hundred acquaintances. I have different communities for different needs. My gaming is to unwind, people I text and call are to keep in touch and connect, and my core friends are the people who get to hear about all the fun or terrible things I am doing.

Finding the right community for me did not happen overnight. I have kicked many people out of my life that were either toxic, (belittling, haters, critics, or bullies), demotivating, constantly gossiping, and constantly making excuses or who just straight up rude or ignorant towards people I care about or people don't even know. The beauty of the internet, and one of the few benefits of social media, is being able to connect with people anywhere at any time, regardless of whether you already know them. If you feel alone or without a community, it takes a little bit of effort, but once you find people who have similar interests, you will naturally make friends. When I played competitive *Call of Duty*, I texted daily with my teammates. One of them lived an hour away, so we met up and played basketball—all because we met randomly on Xbox.

People in Blue Zones live to be over one hundred years old because of the connection they create with each other. Humans are naturally tribal and crave connection. Rachel Naomi Remen, professor of alternative and integrative medicine at the University of California, San Francisco, says it best: "The most basic and powerful way to connect to another person is to listen.[79] Just listen. Perhaps the most important thing we ever give each other is our attention…A loving silence often has far more power to heal and to connect than the most well-intentioned words." Furthermore, the right community is incredibly powerful for your health, and it takes a bit of time to find the right people, but keep searching because there are 7.5 billion people in the world, and you are not alone.

79 Cheryl Payne, "The Most Basic and Powerful Way to Connect to Another Person is to Listen." Mind Journal, Accessed January 26, 2021.

ACTIONS & REFLECTIONS

1. Track everything you eat and drink for a week, and record it in a journal or spreadsheet. Mark how each item made you feel. Reflect on whether or not you need to make nutritional changes. If you want extra assistance, approach a nutritionist or an online community because many people have gone through the process you are about to embark on and have countless learnings.

2. Create a sleep routine. Most importantly, try to go to bed and wake up at the same time every day. When your circadian rhythm is consistent, your body essentially will prepare you for sleep and a natural wake-up time. A big factor of sleeping on time is decreasing digital time 1–2 hours before bed and starting to wind your body down to prepare for sleep.

3. As Blue Zones have taught us, community is a crucial factor to living a lengthy and well life. Find the right community for you, and do not be afraid to try a few to find the right people for you. Never stay attached to a toxic community just because it is convenient.

PART III

CHAPTER 12

EMBRACING THE BECOMING MINDSET AS AN ADOLESCENT

When you are a child with a chronic illness, you often do not understand the full scope of what is going on. The numerous doctor's visits, prescription medication routines, and constantly feeling sick become normal, and you follow what your parents tell you to do. Thankfully, my parents were supportive and made an effort to put my well-being first. I might have gone to the doctor more than the average kid, but I still managed to roam the playground and play sports. Kids feed off of their parents' emotions, and for parents, it can be difficult when their child had a bad day, but showing strength can have a big impact on the child.

Being a diabetic since I was two years old gave me a unique perspective and required me to become an adult more quickly. Suddenly, smaller problems like getting a bad test score did not feel like problems because my health was always the top concern. Ironically, I feel grateful to have struggled so much early on in my life. My pain gave me mental strength and the will to get back up each time after being knocked down. When reflecting on my childhood experience, I think about two Rhode Island high school students who also have chronic illnesses and have become role models for me and others.

OWN YOUR NARRATIVE

Due to COVID, my wife and I left New York City for the suburbs to live with my family in Rhode Island. My neighbor Ryan is a freshman in high school and just turned fifteen years old. We live in a cul-de-sac, so I always see Ryan swinging a golf club or playing basketball, baseball, or football. One day, his mom Kim asked if I wanted to interview him for the book. A look of confusion came over my face because I forgot Ryan had a chronic illness.

Doctors called Ryan a "headache kid." He suffered from headaches often, and his mother kept growing anxious about what this might mean. When the doctor tried to dismiss his pain as something simple, Kim pushed for a second opinion. And thank goodness she did because Ryan really had a brain tumor on his pituitary gland, the part of the brain that impacts hormone production. He was only three years old. To remove the tumor, surgeons went through his nasal cavity, meaning the procedure left no scars.

At first, Kim was a bit nervous because she wanted Ryan to not have a life riddled with challenges, but the doctors in Boston made her feel comfortable. She knew Ryan was in great hands. Having a world-class medical community like the one in Boston only an hour's drive away was a huge advantage to getting the best possible care. If only this level of care and support was available globally.

Ryan took a few pills a day, a nightly injection for his endocrine system, and a biweekly testosterone shot to make sure his body functions as if he had a pituitary gland. The only time Ryan really thought about his tumor was when he received an injection at his yearly MRI. As Ryan says, "Things have gotten easier as I've gotten older. It has been difficult, but the best thing I did was stay positive." That can be hard to do, but when Ryan's friend was diagnosed with ADHD, he started to understand he was not alone. Everyone was going through something.

His mom Kim is extremely attentive in making sure he is doing well. Even when Ryan is fine, Kim always checks in to make sure he is doing okay because she knows it is easy to act tough and hold things in rather than ask for help. Ryan's grandfather was a scientist, so he is always talking about how lucky we are to have medical advancements and how he is able to live the normal life he lives thanks to science.

At school, Ryan was away from his mom, but he had a great support system. His friends all knew about his chronic illness and asked if he took his medications. This was important for Kim because she felt anxiety at times when she was away from her kids. Having your friends not give you a hard time about your condition and being supportive is extremely important. The moment you feel bullied or uncomfortable, you want to avoid school and your friends and prefer to run from your problems and be alone.

A major transition for a child who has a chronic illness tends to happen at the start of high school because you begin to have more say in your doctor's appointments. You become responsible for your medication and choosing to perform or not perform actions that might harm you, such as eating foods that taste good but make you feel terrible after. At age fifteen, Ryan started giving himself his nightly shots. At first, this can be hard because you have to remember to give the injection, to take your medication, and to be more aware of how you are feeling in general.

Ryan's mindset about tackling problems is admirable for an adult and even more so for a teenager. Rather than let the problem negatively impact his mindset, he tries to get in front of it and manage it head on. For example, if he has a long day and cannot sleep, he tries not to think about the events of the day and instead focuses on getting sleep and moving on to the next day. He always keeps pushing forward.

Ryan is in no way ashamed of his condition. He is focused on living in the present, which he believes will positively impact his future. He cannot change any part of what has happened to him or what might happen, so he chooses to own his narrative. Owning his narrative means not being afraid of judgmental people, doing the best you can, and not changing for anyone but yourself.

POWER THROUGH POSITIVITY

My dad Steve is heavily involved in the Rhode Island non-profit sector and is always looking to help people. Eight years ago, my dad connected with Deanna Ayanyan whose daughter Ani was diagnosed with cancer at the age of nine. When I first met Ani, she had lost vision in one eye and lost her hair to chemo, but she was the happiest kid you would ever meet. Her smile would light up the room. Ani was a massive Boston Bruins fan, and since my dad was good friends with hockey player Milan Lucic, we all got together for dinner in Boston. Ani was starstruck, which was funny since everyone else wanted to learn more about her.

After Ani was diagnosed with cancer, Deanna was a bit nervous, but she stayed calm and thought, "We are going to get through this." It is so easy to be negative in this situation and think "Why me?" but positivity is power. Another stressful factor with cancer is how expensive it is to treat; cancer treatment averages $150,000.[80] Ani was preparing for a twelve-hour surgery to remove the tumor. The top doctor, Dr. Cohen, told Deanna he was getting his "A team" together and never asked for insurance, stating, "We will do what we have to do in order to get her healthy."[81] They were in great hands. After the surgery, the nurses formed a deep relationship with Ani. Support during recovery might just be the best medicine because Ani believes that "Rhonda was the best nurse ever. I didn't feel scared or anything. I knew I was

---

80 Peter Moore, "The High Cost of Cancer Treatment," *AARP*, June 1 2018

81 Pam Schiff, "I'm Thankful She Never Lost Hope," Cranston Herald, November 25, 2015.

going to beat it. I would tell other kids to [not] worry about it and be yourself and be strong."

When I asked Ani how she dealt with the diagnosis, doctors, and surgeries at the age of nine, she told me, "I did not really care about anything. I just cared about what was on TV and not what the doctors were doing. Even if I had three IVs in my arm." Ani is insanely tough for a nine-year-old. Her mother told me that Ani has a high tolerance for pain. How did she develop such mental strength?—her mindset towards pain. Ani's attitude built resilience, which made her incredibly strong.

Growing up, Ani was also an athlete. She saw pain as part of the process. Even before Ani had cancer, Deanna instilled such positive values and taught her children that no matter how difficult your life is, you must find ways to think positively and look forward. In the hospital, Ani was allowed to have visitors, and Deanna said, "If you are going to visit Ani and bring negative thoughts or make Ani feel uncomfortable with your staring, you are not welcome." Deanna wanted Ani to know she was normal and wanted to ensure that no one made her feel different.

Many of us struggle to think about the present. Ani doesn't think much about the future of her cancer and focuses on living her best life now. However, she does want to be a graphic designer one day, and I am 1,000 percent confident that whatever Ani sets her mind to, she will achieve.

Ani's nickname is "Wonder Woman" because she is a superhero. She never complains, she stays positive through chemo and radiation, and she refuses to be scared. The only time she really cried as a child was when she and her brother fought. That was it. Her brother Hagop was supportive too, saying, "She was a true warrior through the whole fight, and I'm thankful she never lost hope."

When Ani was nine, she needed proton therapy which required her to wear a face mask and sit still. At the hospital, a seven-year-old boy was having a hard time with the mask. Ani became his mentor. She explained to him how he needed to stay still for the special mask to be molded to his face and head and showed him how she puts her mask on and stays still for the treatment. Numerous families in the community have reached out for support, and Ani always says yes to helping. She understands that having the right support system really does give you the power to be strong and win the battle with your chronic illness.

I am insanely proud of Ani. At first, I was shocked at how casual Ani was about some of her treatments, but it taught me that the patient gets to decide how much pain affects them. No matter how bad things might seem, if you have the right attitude and mindset, you will get through whatever it is you are going through.

ACTIONS & REFLECTIONS

1. Adolescents, adopt the mindset that you are strong and capable of accomplishing anything you set your mind to—because you can. Stay positive.

2. Parents, be there for your child—care, support, and listen. Understand they might not be feeling well, and rather than get frustrated, have empathy. Pain sucks, and you cannot feel what they feel but only hear and see their reactions.

3. For everyone, think about how you can own your narrative. People tend to be judgmental, but do the best you can and love who you are. There is no one else in the world like you. You are unique.

CHAPTER 13

EMBRACING THE BECOMING MINDSET AS AN ADULT

———

When you have your chronic illness under control, you feel on top of the world. You never want to stop making progress, and now that you feel empowered when you feel sick, you look at sickness as a temporary roadblock. Then it is time to get back to enhancing your well-being. In practice, the Becoming Mindset is all about finding what works for you, adapting as your body and environment change, and understanding your well-being is a lifelong journey. It took over twenty years to figure out what works for me because I had no idea what I was doing to my body. Once I finally took action, it took eighteen months to feel incredible. This is the best I have felt in twelve years, and I refuse to go back to the way I was.

IT TOOK A PANDEMIC TO GET ON TRACK

I thought 2020 was going to be the greatest year of my life. Work was going well, we booked tickets to the Tokyo Olympics, and we were supposed to get married and start planning for a family. In reality, I was laid off, we did not have a wedding, the Olympics were postponed, and we delayed any talks of having kids. The year 2020 sucked for everyone, but how did I still find joy through the madness?

Despite all the letdowns, including multiple job offers not coming to fruition, there was still so much to be grateful for. I was given the time to write this book and time to put health first, and my family is healthy. I always claimed to put my health first, but I was lying to myself. Prior to March 2020, I felt functional. By December 2020, I felt functionally well—time to thrive.

The world was out of control in 2020—a global pandemic, a divided country, and all types of natural disasters. I decided to focus on what I could control: me. I stopped watching the news, deleted my social media apps, and had the discipline to watch no more than two episodes of *Game of Thrones* in a single day. I also started building a daily routine.

I was always against making a routine, but I soon enough realized the power of consistency. Waking up, sleeping, eating, and going for a walk at the same time added much-needed structure to my day. My health was finally first. To ensure I was eating right, I subscribed to a service with a company called Kencko, which provides ground-up fruits and vegetables for smoothies. Getting the right nutrients, or fuel, helped give me the energy to get through the day feeling well. A major lesson in this process was that actions have consequences. The moment I cut out snacking and studied what foods had a positive or negative impact on my stomach and glucose levels, my wellness continued to improve.

The most important part of my health journey was building awareness. I had no idea that any of these strategies existed or helped people feel better. I continuously evaluated what I learned, worked with doctors, built a support system, and trained my mindset. Now, I am focused on strengthening the relationship between holistic and traditional medicine via lifestyle changes. My health is an ongoing medical experiment where I am the doctor because I know my body better than anyone, and it is my job to take care of it.

I am making progress. I am able to sleep throughout the night, my stomach indigestion is mostly gone, and my ninety-day glucose average is below 125 mg/dL, which could prevent further health complications from diabetes down the road. It took years to feel this well, but through determination, patience, and learning the right strategies, it is happening. And it is well worth it.

If I let diabetes control me, I can experience stomach problems, insomnia, stress, and many other health problems. If I attack the problem at the source, I have control and power over my body. Having control over your body is a long-term way of thinking. Years ago, I felt fine, so I assumed that what I was doing was working. However, far too many diabetics wait to care about their disease management until they have had a foot amputated, start to lose their vision, or begin to have organ failure. In order to live a long, healthy life, you need to put in the work and have a long-term plan. It takes discipline, lifestyle changes, and finding what works for you, but you can make it work. Just don't give up. You got this.

LIVING YOUR BEST LIFE

The only time Paola remembers that she has Crohn's is on Sunday when she takes her weekly Humira injection. Since my mom has Crohn's, I asked if she had any advice for Paola, and she said that medical marijuana took her off Humira and reduced her daily pills from more than twenty to zero. Maybe this will help Paola get off of Humira since she wants kids and cannot take Humira while pregnant. At the very least, it gives her something to research and another potential option for treatment.

I don't have Crohn's, but I do have gastroparesis, and one of the most helpful tips Paola shared concerns breathing. It sounds straightforward, but breathing is crucial to your well-being. When she is calm, she has no Crohn's flare-ups, her stress is down, and her overall health feels better. We both meditate, and it helps immensely. Especially when you are doing blood work or about to take a painful shot, focus on your breathing rather than the needle, and you will be surprisingly calm.

Another mindset shift Paola exhibited was thinking about the long term. She knows that if she does not take care of herself, Crohn's could eventually lead to colon cancer or an ostomy bag.[82] Paola goes on frequent long-distance hikes while knowing her limits and has found the right diet that makes her feel good. She once went hiking in Seattle with a few hardcore hikers, and they were aware of Paola's Crohn's, allowing her to lead the group at her pace. She surrounds herself with the right people, and her boyfriend is always there for her too. If you were to compare Paola when I first met her to who she is now, you would see a stark difference. In her own words, "I am a much better version of myself because I am more conscious of how to better take care of me."

A major lifestyle change Paola made was finding the best work environment. She worked for the World Bank and was constantly on a plane and traveling, which can definitely be stressful. Although she loved it, she needed to slow down and joined a tech company in San Francisco that has a very supportive culture. If she is struggling and needs the day off to address her Crohn's, her manager understands and, without question, lets her get the rest she needs. Luckily, she's only had to do this once. So many of us know our limits, yet we push boundaries to try and work. Slow down, and take the time to rest.

Lastly, Paola taught me about how lonely pain can be. Every Sunday when she injects Humira, her boyfriend is by her side and holds her arm, but it is still a lonely experience. Sometimes loneliness is a blessing because you are the only one who can do something about it but a curse because only you can relate to how much pain you are experiencing. Paola's

---

82   "What is an Ostomy," United Ostomy Association of America, accessed January 27, 2021.

biggest tip is to find a way to get comfortable with the process, especially after blood work and injections. One way she did this was by getting a tattoo on her left wrist which reads "audentes fortuna juvat," Latin for "fortune favors the bold." Whenever she looks at the tattoo, she feels strong, even if she feels alone.

I HAVE MS, BUT MS DOES NOT HAVE ME

During my freshman year of college, I met Kevin Hoegler who was full of life and is one of the fittest people I have ever known. A few weeks later, Kevin was on a treadmill and started to feel numb from the waist down. He went to the emergency room, and the doctor said it was only inflammation in his spine. A neurologist then performed a test to see if Kevin could tell which toe he was moving. He had no idea, which was alarming and led to a series of tests. Kevin went to a specialist in New Jersey and found out he had thirty lesions in his brain and spine. He was diagnosed with multiple sclerosis (MS), which can be disabling disease of the brain and spinal cord and, if not controlled, can cause serious health problems.

Kevin's diagnosis was difficult to process. College was a new environment, and he had the mentality of "Why is this happening to me?" which he soon realized was the wrong mindset. He stopped going to parties, avoided the gym, and felt like MS held him back. The best medicine was breathing because it calmed him down. Thinking about his health, friends, sports, and school was overwhelming. Kevin's mindset changed when he realized he did not have to figure out the entirety of his life at that moment. He decided to take a step back to figure out what worked for him, and slowing down his pace created comfort.

Kevin had a supportive family which allowed him to still have a great college experience. He found ways to go to parties with friends, play rugby, and be involved on campus. After college, he joined the board of directors for the New Jersey chapter of the National MS Society.

As Kevin grew up and became more educated about MS, he learned to not take things at face value because life does not have a predetermined path. For example, Kevin might have MS, but that does not mean he will constantly be at the doctor's office and taking medication his entire life. Kevin decided to manifest his own destiny and play rugby, work, and listen to his body. Biofeedback—what your body says to your brain—helped Kevin have a healthy relationship with his MS. If you are tired, go to bed. If you are stressed, take a break. If your knee hurts from running, stop running and stretch or ice your knee. Ultimately, biofeedback helps you create boundaries around what works and where you need to take a step back.

The remaining two areas that have changed Kevin's life over the last few years are how he works with doctors and how he manages nutrition. Kevin views his MS doctor as a resource. He takes a few tests annually, talks through the results with his doctor, and consults on his options. His doctor told him that without his medication, his well-being could deteriorate, although Kevin wants to eventually get off of his medicine. I think the doctor should create a path for him to get off his medication as an option. Kevin feels he is 95 percent of the way there because he has improved his lifestyle, nutrition, and mindset.

Since Kevin was fit and always at the gym, he thought he knew a lot about nutrition. Once he started reading books by nutritionists, listening to stories about diets of those with MS, and doing his own research, he realized he had a lot to learn. Eating whole foods instead of processed foods and even going vegan for a year changed the way Kevin thought about food. Food is fuel, and if you want your body to run at its highest level, you need the best fuel.

Through nutritional research, Kevin also realized the importance of routine, which I have now realized too. For Kevin this meant bed at 9:30 p.m., wake up at 5:25 a.m., and then go for a run and go to the gym. When you sleep well, you are happier, less stressed, and more ready for the day. Fixing this one problem is a game changer. When I had chronic insomnia, it was hard to smile after a terrible night of waking up multiple times. As Kevin says, "You need to realize that not getting a lot of sleep is going to be linked to your symptoms, and eating a bowl of garbage for breakfast is going to cause you to be more tired. The more tired you are, the more stress. The more stress, the more flare-ups." This cycle can spiral out of control and adversely affect your overall health and well-being.

Lastly, let's talk about holistic health. Kevin found what works for him from a nutritional, routine and an exercise standpoint. It can take years to establish, but once in place, such routines can really pay off. Finding what works for you takes discipline, respect for your own well-being, and trial and error. When people hear the term "holistic health," for some reason they tend to think of someone who lives in Tibet for a year and studies Buddhism. In reality, holistic health is about looking at your health as a whole and seeing the long-term picture. Eating healthy, going for a thirty-minute walk a day, taking a few deep breaths when you are stressed, or creating a routine that helps you sleep at night are all elements of a holistically healthy life. Want to walk for ten minutes or an hour per day? Cool, do what works for you. Be open-minded in finding a solution because growth can be uncomfortable, especially at first. Finding what works for you takes time, and patience is a part of the process. Human beings tend to be reluctant to change, but change is a powerful tool to keep pushing forward.

Paola, Kevin, and I have learned many lessons about becoming functionally well, but this is not the end of the road. You can train your mind not to be dominated by illness or pain, but you will still face a lifelong journey. Once you get to this stage, you must keep pushing forward because feeling well requires practice, patience, and mental strength. Once you have adopted the Becoming Mindset, it is your time to help someone else start the journey to feeling well.

ACTIONS & REFLECTIONS

1. Work in short ten-minute breaks every hour, and take time to exercise. Even a walk around the neighborhood or outside of the office will do. Keep your body moving, and give it time to relax to avoid stress.

2. Do your research. People have done what you are trying to do, so there is a lot to be learned, and then you can apply what makes sense to you. If you need help, ask the community to get feedback on what you are interested in learning more about.

3. Understand that the Becoming Mindset requires discipline, lifestyle changes, and finding what works best for you. Start small and track your experiments to measure how you are progressing.

CHAPTER 14

EMBRACING THE BECOMING MINDSET IN A SUPPORT ROLE

———

You might be among the four in ten Americans who do not have a chronic illness and are wondering, "Well, how can I be supportive?" [83] Throughout this book, you have heard about the power of community, family, and friends and how the right support system can make living with a chronic illness much easier. One of the important bricks in the foundation of support involves knowing how to be there for someone in a time of need. I want to share ten practical tips for those who might be friends, family members, or just plain curious about how to truly be there for someone with a chronic illness.

———

83 "Chronic Disease in America," National Center for Chronic Disease Prevention and Health Promotion, accessed February 8, 2021.

BEING JUDGMENTAL IS NOT COOL

Being sick and feeling well are not mutually exclusive. Like Kevin Hoegler, you might have multiple sclerosis but still feel incredibly functional and well. This is why it can be difficult for someone experiencing internal pain because those around us have no idea what we are going through. Most pain is not visible, which is why we shouldn't make any assumptions. If someone uses glasses for vision, a wheelchair to gain mobility, or an insulin pump for diabetes, you can gauge that extra support is needed. But for the pain you cannot see, you probably won't know that support is needed. We can all practice being kind and respectful. It goes a long way. Listen to your thoughts, think before you speak, and assess if what you are saying has the right phrasing and tone. Consider a conversation as an opportunity to learn. Did you find that your comments landed negatively? Perhaps take a few seconds prior to speaking to practice active listening.

BEING UNCOMFORTABLE IS OKAY

Whether injecting insulin at the dinner table or stretching my legs on a flight from knee pain, I often receive weird looks. Staring at anyone can cause discomfort for that person because it makes them seem different than everyone else. People often ask me about my diabetes, and I am always happy to educate anyone interested in learning. Just be nice when you ask and show that you want to learn more. Awareness and exposure are excellent ways towards building a more inclusive society. If you have never seen a diabetic inject insulin, someone blackout due to a seizure, or a patient with a PICC line in their arm, you might feel uncomfortable. That is okay. The person you are interacting with is a human being too, just like you. Their pain does not define who they are, and you may never walk in their shoes, but the effort to understand will show that you are capable of empathy.

ALL PAIN IS NOT EQUAL

It can be really difficult to relate to someone's pain because even if you can see or hear their struggles, you can never feel exactly what they feel. Pain impacts us all differently, and we have to respect that fact. Blood work is something most of us go through. Some people pass out; others sit there and check their email while ten vials of blood are taken. Remember that we are all unique, and that is perfectly fine.

EXPECTATIONS CAN LEAD TO DISAPPOINTMENT

As a kid, I was hospitalized four times for various stomach bugs. After these visits, my parents felt I was magically healed and expected me to go back to school once I was able to start eating again. No way. Feeling functional requires a few days of rest because hospital beds are uncomfortable and the medications need time to work. Also, the stress of catching up on schoolwork and rushing back to class made me feel worse. Arguing to stay home was not easy, but it had to be done. My doctors expected me to be back to "normal" life in two days, but based on what? There were times where a few days' rest were definitely needed, and there were situations where I physically felt fine but was not mentally prepared. Expecting something to happen that does not come to fruition often leads to feelings of disappointment—in this case, for my parents. If someone you love needs time, do your best to be there for them. Showing someone you care for them is great medicine. Build trust and understanding by listening to their needs and being supportive rather than telling them how they feel.

PAIN IS NOT ALL IN YOUR HEAD

Do you know someone who is constantly in pain? A good friend of mine, Greg, is in his early thirties and had two major spinal surgeries in the last year. When you talk to Greg, he laughs and jokes and is incredibly smart. Behind the enthusiasm is a man searching for answers to his pain. Many people never really understood how much pain he was in. Doctors even said that the pain was all in his head. But it is not. Only the person in pain truly knows how much pain they are in, and it is hard for others to relate because they cannot feel the person's pain. With that being said, it is difficult to compare pain from one person to another since each person handles pain differently. Be kind. Be empathetic. Listen.

JUST BECAUSE YOU AREN'T AFFECTED DOES NOT MEAN IT DOES NOT MATTER

I often hear people say, "my taxes are too high, and I am healthy, so why am I subsidizing health care for those who are sick?" For the chronically ill, health care bills are way too high. Annually, direct health care costs for a patient with chronic disease average $6,032, approximately five times that of a person without a chronic disease.[84] Even if

---

84 Tara. O'Neill Hayes, et al., "Chronic Disease in the United States: A Worsening Health and Economic Crisis," *American Action Forum*, September 10, 2020.

you are not directly impacted, these expenses likely affect people you love and care about. Many of us do not get to choose whether we have a chronic illness or not. Pieces of legislation like the Affordable Care Act are important because they allow people with preexisting conditions to receive health care. Putting health first is good for our society because the healthier we are, the more productive we can be. As mentioned earlier, you should care because six in ten Americans have a chronic illness, and these people are your family members, friends, and members of your community. If it does not affect you, it impacts the people around you.

BE A THOUGHTFUL FRIEND

Due to my gastroparesis, I adopted a vegetarian diet in 2016. The kindest thing my friends do for me is ensuring that there are at least three vegetarian options at a restaurant that I can choose from. Whether it is Paola's friends letting her lead the way on a hike or Emily Lemiska's friends letting her have a bed during a camping trip, showing empathy and respect is the best thing anyone can do for a friend. For example, say, "I don't understand how you are feeling, but I respect it, and I will do what I can to make things easier for you." When you take thoughtful action, however small, you make a big impact on someone's life. That is why surrounding yourself with the right people is so crucial to feeling well.

IF WE "FLAKE," IT MAY MEAN WE NEEDED THE REST

People often use the word "flake" when a friend bails on hanging out. However, this might happen when your chronically ill friend has a bad flare-up, starts feeling sick out of nowhere, or just needs some time alone. We are each in charge of our life and the decisions we make. If someone chooses to do something, respect their wishes. I know you want to spend time with your friend, and I am sure they want to hang out with you, but it is not always that simple. On top of that, maybe they don't want to tell you all of the details of why they cannot attend. A simple "no worries, we hope you feel better, and let's chat when you are feeling better" will go a long way. Be kind.

SHARE YOUR STORY, BUT LISTEN TOO

A few years back, one of my roommates walked into the apartment with a sad look on his face. We asked what was going on, and he told us that his mom passed away from cancer. She was sick for a year, so we were aware of the situation but were still hurt. We were supportive, gave him a hug, and asked about how his family was handling the news. After a few minutes, the conversation became quiet, so I thought sharing a similar story might create comfort. I told him about how my grandfather passed away from cancer and reflected on the good times we had together rather than focusing on the cancer killing him. He appreciated it, but I know it was equally as important to be a strong listener and ensure he felt supported. Afterward, we would frequently check in to ensure he was doing okay. When someone shares a personal story with you, they are being vulnerable and trusting you. Listen to what they have to say because they want you to truly listen and need you to be there for them.

DO YOUR RESEARCH

Taking the time and effort to better understand someone shows how much you care. Recently, on a call with someone I just met, we spoke about diabetes and my book. I found it impressive when he asked questions about the different types of diabetes and knew some high-level information. You can use resources from nonprofits, watch YouTube videos about a patient's experience, and read blogs discussing the right language to use, what a specific chronic illness entails from a diagnosis and treatment standpoint, and how to be supportive—like this book. However, it is key to not seem like an expert after twenty minutes of research, especially when talking to someone who has had a chronic illness for years or most of their life. Overall, look at each conversation as a learning experience, and you will always walk away with new information. Show genuine curiosity that displays that you care and want to learn. Do not assume you know everything about an illness.

ACTIONS & REFLECTIONS

1. Text someone you know who has been struggling lately and let them know that you care. All you have to do is let them know you are thinking about them. It will make their day.
2. Think before you speak. Your words carry weight, so use them wisely.
3. Reflect on a time you were around someone in pain. Were the people around you supportive? If not, how can you be supportive the next time you are in a similar situation?

CONCLUSION

———

Thank you for embarking on this journey about turning pain into power. Adopting the Becoming Mindset and living a healthy life is a process and requires self-reflection and long-term thinking. At the end of each chapter, I put a few actions to take. Ideas are cool, but without action, ideas are just words. All of the tips, advice, and actions to take can feel very overwhelming at first. So how do you actually start to utilize the Becoming Mindset and spring into action? Here are my recommendations.

SHARE YOUR STORY

Everyone has a story. Yes, even you. Being comfortable enough to tell a single person or the whole world your story is powerful because those thoughts you had in your head will suddenly be out there for someone to listen to and respond to. To get comfortable, write it down and make some edits. Don't think. Be authentic, and share it all. Think of yourself as an unedited video, because in today's world, we care way too much about the edited and filtered versions of ourselves. Just be you. Once you have your story, share it with someone you feel comfortable speaking with—a close friend, a family member, a community forum, a nonprofit organization, your therapist. I am an open book, and I share all of my stories because I want you to know you are not alone. It allows me to connect with you as a fellow human being.

BUILD A PLAN

On brendanbarbato.com you will find a template to help you build custom plans for yourself. When building a plan, there are four important things to remember. First, do not be afraid to fail. Failure is where our best learnings come from and is a part of life. The point is not to be a perfectionist. Plans take time and evolve often, which brings me to my second point: Do not be afraid to pivot. If you are trying to learn to love vegetables for the first time, try something different. Not everyone likes broccoli, but maybe you like brussel sprouts or corn. Third, trial and error are key. You need to take the time necessary to find what works for you. Lastly, be patient. You are essentially running an experiment, and it takes time to create the right formula for your body. Building a plan allows you to push forward and take action. I also recommend an accountability buddy so you have someone to check in with.

FIND THE RIGHT ENVIRONMENT

Trying to enhance your sleep habits when your friend group goes clubbing three times per week or your diet when everyone around you constantly eats fast food is a nightmare. Humans are tribal, and we tend to act similarly to those we surround ourselves with. You do not have to kick people out of your life—unless they are toxic—but you can expand your environment and join different friend groups. I have my diabetes, LEGO sets, Fortnite, work, and childhood friend groups. You need to allocate time where your priorities are. It can be incredibly difficult to suddenly just leave an environment. You can start distancing yourself by reaching out less or simply saying, "Hey, you are my friends, but I need to work on me right now, so I am going to do some exploring." If they understand, you have great friends, and if you get made fun of, they are unsupportive, and you are likely better off without them. I plan to create a community so anyone who reads this book can be matched with a group of people also searching for accountability, support, and friends.

BREATHE

The box breathing technique teaches us to breathe in for four seconds, hold for four seconds, breathe out for four seconds, and hold for four seconds.[85] Breathing is one of the most powerful mechanisms for relieving stress, focusing, and putting your mind at ease. When you are relaxed and are well, you probably feel on top of the world. I know I do. For example, every time before I do blood work, I breathe in and then out as the needle goes in. I am relaxed, and even if the nurse is taking ten vials of blood, I stay pretty calm. Meditation is an amazing practice and can take as little as ten minutes per day to be effective. Breathing is incredible medicine.

---

85   Deborah Weatherspoon, "Box Breathing," *Healthline*, June 17, 2020.

FIND EQUILIBRIUM

Have quick highs and lows. When things are going well, do not over celebrate. When things are going poorly, do not sulk for too long. The more you can be in equilibrium, the better you will feel because your emotions are more stable. The best way to be in equilibrium is to take a deep breath and reset.

TAKE ACTION

Saying you are going to do something is easy. Doing it is the hard part, and so is changing your behavior. If you have had Crohn's disease, Lyme disease, or spinal pain your entire life, simply changing your habits one day is difficult but certainly possible. While some people can become vegetarian overnight, others may require months of trial and error. Any pace is good as long as you are headed in the right direction. The best way to change is to think about the long-term impact of your decisions. What will change enable you to do that you cannot do now?—sleep better, feel well, and decrease pain? Whatever it is, use it as your north star, and keep pushing forward.

I am beyond excited for you to embark on a journey of self-discovery and finding what works for you. I want you to live your best life, and I believe in you to make it happen.

ACKNOWLEDGEMENTS

———

No one succeeds alone. I am grateful to have countless incredible human beings in my corner.

I want to thank the following people:

First, the MVP of life partners, Eiko, for her support. She is the best.

The amazing individuals I interviewed for this book and learned from: Emily Lemiska, Tiffany Yu, Kevin Hoegler, Jacqueline Calamia, Ashanti Branch, Ryan Newton, Ani Ayanyan, and Paola Cordovez.

My beta readers went above and beyond and gave me incredible feedback. They helped me rewrite the book multiple times and make each version better than the last. Thank you Eiko Tsukamoto, Jenn Hourani, Paola Cordovez, Arjun Rajesh, and Mary Ann Dailey.

Thank you, New Degree Press and the legendary Eric. I could not have done this without you. Thank you, Cameron, Jacqueline, and Kathy.

Shout out to the 150 early backers who believed in me and preordered this book.

Tyler Amaral, Heather Arora, Sean Arroyo, Kristen Assalone, Abdilahi Bade, Sandra Baker, Gloria Balderas, Jonathan Ball, Kyle Barbato, Steven Barbato, Kim Barbato, John Barbosa, Gavin Bauman, John Birchall, Todd Birmingham, Mark Blair, Simon Boehme, Margaret Boland, Raymond Bolvin, Dianne Brause, Evan Broccoli, Mike Broccoli, Michael Broccoli, Kim Cavanaugh, Andrew Coca, Paola Cordovez, Tony Corrente, Thomas Cui, Mary Ann Dailey, Brennan Dailey, Tyler Davey, Frank DeCosta III, Keryn Deighan, Paula DeRuosi, Richie Doyle, Thomas Escobar, Daniel Estrada, Carey Fan, Michelle Ferri, Andrew Foley, Aimee Gagnon, Mary Gale, Dillon Galynsky, Dylan Gambardella, Benjamin Gavin, Gail Gavin, Maggie Gendron, Sueja Goldhahn, Alex Grant, Kevin Gryspeerd, Alexandra Harbour, Daniel Hernandez, Antonette Ho, Jennifer Hourani, Rilwan Ilumoka, Tyler Inkley, Allison Jernigan, David Jessen, Sean Jonckheere, Nate Jones, Phil Jones, Gil Kazimirov, Mark Keenan, Brian Kilroy, Brexton Kinney, Eric Koester, Alex Krasnoff, Chris Kroft, Michelle Laliberte, Ben LaRocco, Salvatore Laurito, Kyle Lawson, Feebee Lee, Chao Li, Michelle Loiselle, Derek Lombardi, Hari Mahesh, Danny Mallette, Joel Mampilly, Jonathan Marchetti, Lauren Mariano, Madeline Martini, Karen Martufi, Doreen Masciarelli, Michelle McCormick, Steven McKendall, David Mok, Michael Mozer, Sreeram Mullankandy, Kim Newton, Larry NG, Denis Novak, Ben

Ortega, Anthony Ottone, Jeanine Palleschi, Linda Palmiotti, Rachel Pardue, Neetal Parekh, Tony Paske, Richard Patenaude, Paula Pepe, Jonathan Perri, Stephanie Potts, Judy Pratt, Colber Prosper, Flora Qu, Jenny Quenard, Arjun Rajesh, Brianne Reardon, Dennis Reardon, Mikey Regan, Benjamin Ricci, Cameron Ricci, Rob Rizzo, Todd Rizzo, Cynthia Robinson Dasilva, Jennifer Rocha, Sam & Pam Romanella, Benjamin Rubenstein, Conor Ryan, Ben Sack, Josh Sandin, Brandon Schwartz, Benjamin Schwartzman, Michael Scott, Jared Silver, Kerry Silvia, Nathan Slinn, William Smith, Scott Soares, Hannah Sorila, Paul Spetrini, Evan Stamps, Scott Stump, Brett Swanson, Jennifer Taliani, Terri Tasca, Evan Teitelbaum, Ian Thiel, Ted Tobiason, Lauren Tokushige, Connie Truong, Camy Tsukamoto, Eiko Tsukamoto, Angela Tsung, Derek Tu, Robert Varr, Partha Vasisht, Rachel Walker, Daniel Walkup, Jianhan Wang, Steven Wawryk, Jason Wilde, Lloyd Winston, Michael Wisdom, Ann Wong, John Yeaman, Alex Youn, and Gregory "The Man" Ziemak

Lastly, I want to thank **YOU** for going on this incredible journey with me. I am proud of you and cannot wait to hear about all of your incredible progress.

APPENDIX

———

INTRODUCTION

Canadian Mental Health Association. "The Relationship between Mental Health, Mental Illness and Chronic Physical Conditions." Accessed October 6, 2020. https://ontario.cmha.ca/documents/the-relationship-between-mental-health-mental-illness-and-chronic-physical-conditions/

Lim, Catherine, Andrew B.L. Berry, Tad Hirsch, Andrea L. Hartzler, Edward H. Wagner, Evette Ludman, and James D. Ralston. "'It just seems outside my health': How Patients with Chronic Conditions Perceive Communication Boundaries with Providers." *Designing Interactive Systems (Conference)* 2016 (2016): 1172–1184. doi:10.1145/2901790.2901866.

National Center for Chronic Disease Prevention and Health Promotion. "Chronic Disease in America." Accessed October 6, 2020. https://www.cdc.gov/chronicdisease/resources/infographic/chronic-diseases.htm

Wilson, Laurnie. "Asking for Help May Be a Privilege." *CivicScience.* September 13, 2018. https://civicscience.com/asking-for-help-may-be-a-privilege/

CHAPTER 1

American Diabetes Association. "The History of a Wonderful Thing We Call Insulin." Accessed November 2, 2020. https://www.diabetes.org/blog/history-wonderful-thing-we-call-insulin#:~:text=In%201921%2C%20a%20young%20surgeon, millions%20of%20people%20with%20diabetes.

Centers for Disease Control and Prevention, US Department of Health & Human Services. "National Diabetes Statistics Report 2020." Accessed November 2, 2020. https://www.cdc. gov/diabetes/library/features/diabetes-stat-report.html#:~: text=Key%20findings%20include%3A,Asians%20and%20 non%2DHispanic%20whites.

Centers for Disease Control and Prevention. "Number of Americans with Diabetes Projected to Double or Triple by 2050." Accessed November 2, 2020. https://www.cdc.gov/ media/pressrel/2010/r101022.html#:~:text=As%20many%20 as%201%20in,U.S.%20adults%20has%20diabetes%20now.

Healthline Media Inc. "Diabetes: Facts, Statistics, and You." Accessed November 2, 2020. https://www.healthline.com/ health/diabetes/facts-statistics-infographic#:~:text=With%20 type%201%20diabetes%2C%20the,year%20in%20the%20 United%20States

Healthline Media Inc. "Type 1 and Type 2 Diabetes: What's the Difference?" Accessed November 2, 2020. https://www.healthline. com/health/difference-between-type-1-and-type-2-diabetes #risk-factors

O'Neill, Hayes, Tara, Josee Farmer. "Insulin Cost and Pricing Trends." American Action Forum. April 2, 2020. https://www. americanactionforum.org/research/insulin-cost-and-pricing-trends/

Sifferlin, Alexandra. "There's Hope for a Vaccine to Prevent Type 1 Diabetes." *Time,* June 21, 2018. https://time.com/5318733/ vaccine-type-1-diabetes/

CHAPTER 2

BlueCross Blueshield. "Why does healthcare cost so much?" Accessed November 10, 2020. https://www.bcbs.com/issues-indepth/why-does-healthcare-cost-so-much

Centers for Disease Control and Prevention. "About Prediabetes & Type 2 Diabetes." Accessed November 10, 2020.https://www. cdc.gov/diabetes/prevention/about-prediabetes.html#:~:text= Diabetes%20Is%20Serious%20and%20Common&text=An%20 additional%2088%20million%20U.S.,be%20considered%20 type%202%20diabetes.

Davis, Scott. "LeBron James Reportedly Spends $1.5 Million Per Year To Take Care of His Body." *Business Insider,* July 29, 2018. https://www.businessinsider.com/how-lebron-james-spends-money-body-care-2018-7

Centers for Disease Control and Prevention. "Health and Economic Costs of Chronic Diseases." Accessed November 10, 2020.https://www.cdc.gov/chronicdisease/about/costs/index. htm

Centers for Disease Control and Prevention. "Health Expenditures." Accessed November 10, 2020.https://www.cdc.gov/nchs/ fastats/health-expenditures.htm

CNBC. "32% of American Workers Have Medical Debt—and Over Half Have Defaulted On it." Accessed November 10, 2020. https://www.cnbc.com/2020/02/13/one-third-of-american-workers-have-medical-debt-and-most-default.html

"Health Care in Germany: The German Health Care System." Institute for Quality and Efficiency in Health Care 2006. https:// www.ncbi.nlm.nih.gov/books/NBK298834/HeartMath. "How Stress Affects the Body." Accessed November 10, 2020. https:// app.box.com/s/xm6wq1nb6rcmpdqy8l48mv20duprr495

Howard, Jenny. "Plague was one of history's deadliest diseases— then we found a cure." *National Geographic*, July 6, 2020. https://www.nationalgeographic.com/science/health-and-human-body/human-diseases/the-plague/#close

Keisler-Starkey, Katherine, Lisa N. Bunch. "Health Insurance Coverage in the United States: 2019." *United States Census Bureau*. September 15, 2020 https://www.census.gov/library/ publications/2020/demo/p60-271.html

Leonhardt, Megan. "Nearly 1 in 4 Americans are Skipping Medical Care Because of the Cost." *CNBC*. March 12 2020. https://www.

cnbc.com/2020/03/11/nearly-1-in-4-americans-are-skipping-medical-care-because-of-the-cost.htmlMachlin, Steven R., Emily M. Mitchell. "Expenses for Office-Based Physician Visits by Specialty and Insurance Type 2016." Agency for Healthcare Research and Quality. October 2018. https://meps.ahrq.gov/data_files/publications/st517/stat517.shtml#:~:text=While%20the%20overall%20mean%20expense,physician%20specialty%20than%20mean%20expenses.

Roser, Max, Esteban Ortiz-Ospina, and Hannah Ritchie. "Life Expectancy," Our World in Data. October 2019. https://ourworldindata.org/life-expectancy

RxSaver. "How Much Do Antibiotics Cost Without Insurance?" Accessed November 10, 2020. https://rxsaver.retailmenot.com/blog/how-much-do-antibiotics-cost-without-insurance

Study.com. "Becoming a Doctor in the US: Medical School, Residency & Licensing Requirements." Accessed November 10, 2020. https://study.com/requirements_to_become_a_doctor.html#:~:text=The%20requirements%20for%20becoming%20a,are%20eligible%20for%20medical%20licensing.

TEDxTalks. "Ashkan Fardost: A Cure for No Cure: The Next Generation of Medicine." October 14, 2015. Video, 14:17. https://www.youtube.com/watch?v=W3C23m71Yws

The History of Vaccines. "Vaccine Development, Testing and Regulation." Accessed November 10, 2020. https://www.historyofvaccines.org/content/articles/vaccine-development-testing-and-regulation

CHAPTER 3

Advanced Tissue. "How Sleep Deprivation Negatively Impacts Wound Healing." Accessed December 15, 2020. https://advancedtissue.com/2017/04/sleep-deprivation-negatively-impacts-wound-healinghow-sleep-deprivation-negatively-impacts-wound-healing/#:~:text=It%20directly%20impacts%20your%20immune%20system&text=Health%20Line%20explained%20that%20when,healing%20time%20and%20developing%20infections.

Canadian Mental Health Association. "The Relationship Between Mental Health, Mental Illness and Chronic Physical Conditions." Accessed December 15, 2020. https://ontario.cmha.ca/documents/the-relationship-between-mental-health-mental-illness-and-chronic-physical-conditions/#:~:text=are%20fundamentally%20linked.-,People%20living%20with%20a%20serious%20mental%20illness%20are%20at%20higher,rate%20of%20the%20general%20population.

Kiesel, Laura. "Chronic Pain: The Invisible Disability." *Harvard Health Publishing* (blog). April 28, 2017. https://www.health.harvard.edu/blog/chronic-pain-the-invisible-disability-2017042811360

Khatri, Minesh. "What is H. Pylori?" *WebMD*. December 7, 2020. https://www.webmd.com/digestive-disorders/h-pylori-helicobacter-pylori#1

Krishnasamy Sathya, Abell TL. "Diabetic Gastroparesis: Principles and Current Trends in Management." *Diabetes Ther*. 2018. 1-42. doi: 10.1007/s13300-018-0454-9Mayo Foundation for Medical Education and Research. "Crohn's Disease."

Accessed December 15, 2020. https://www.mayoclinic.org/diseases-conditions/crohns-disease/diagnosis-treatment/drc-20353309#:~:text=There%20is%20currently%20no%20cure,term%20prognosis%20by%20limiting%20complications.

TEDxTalks. "Amy Morin: The Secret of Becoming Mentally Strong." December 4, 2015. Video. https://www.youtube.com/watch?v=TFbv757kup4&list=PLFZCIOS7DCUgBpmxj_kmVjCBaHSCZaMT7&index=7&t=0s

CHAPTER 4

American Diabetes Association. "The Cost of Diabetes." Accessed December 17, 2020. https://www.diabetes.org/resources/statistics/cost-diabetes#:~:text=The%20estimated%20total%20economic%20cost,that%20diabetes%20imposes%20on%20society.

Centers for Medicare & Medicaid Services. "Historical." Accessed December 10, 2020. https://www.cms.gov/Research-Statistics-Data-and-Systems/Statistics-Trends-and-Reports/NationalHealthExpendData/NationalHealthAccountsHistorical#:~:text=U.S.%20health%20care%20spending%20grew,spending%20accounted%20for%2017.7%20percent.

Szalavitz, Maia. "Why Swearing Sparingly Can Help Kill Pain." *Time*, November 23, 2011. https://healthland.time.com/2011/11/23/why-swearing-sparingly-can-help-kill-pain/#:~:text=It%20seems%20that%20swearing%20may,drugs%20like%20morphine%20and%20oxycodone.

CHAPTER 5

American Academy of Orthopedic Surgeons. "Osgood–Schlatter Disease." Accessed November 21, 2020. https://orthoinfo.aaos. org/en/diseases--conditions/osgood-schlatter-disease-knee-pain/

Barre, Prasad Vijay., Padmaja Gadiraju, Suvashisa Rana, S., & Tiamongla. "Stress and Quality of Life in Cancer Patients: Medical and Psychological Intervention." *Indian journal of psychological medicine*, vol. 40.3 (2018) 232–238. https://doi. org/10.4103/IJPSYM.IJPSYM_512_17

Chapman University. "America's Top Fears 2017." Accessed December 1, 2020. https://blogs.chapman.edu/wilkinson/2017/10/11/ americas-top-fears-2017/

Mayo Clinic. "Grand mal seizure." Accessed November 6, 2020. https://www.mayoclinic.org/diseases-conditions/grand-mal-seizure/symptoms-causes/syc-20363458#:~:text=A%20 grand%20mal%20seizure%20causes,electrical%20activity%20 throughout%20the%20brain.

Nuffield Trust & The Health Foundation. "Cancer Survival Rates." Accessed December 13, 2020. https://www.nuffieldtrust.org.uk/ resource/cancer-survival-rates

CHAPTER 6

Centers for Disease Control and Prevention. "Learn About Mental Health," Centers for Disease Control and Prevention. Accessed November 11, 2020. https://www.cdc.gov/ mentalhealth/learn/index.htm#:~:text=More%20than%20

50%25%20will%20be,some%20point%20in%20their%20 lifetime.&text=1%20in%205%20Americans%20will,illness%20 in%20a%20given%20year.

Cigna. "Loneliness is at Epidemic Levels in America." Accessed November 11, 2020. https://www.cigna.com/about-us/ newsroom/studies-and-reports/combatting-loneliness/

Clarke, Emilia. "A Battle for My Life." *The New Yorker*. March 21, 2019, https://www.newyorker.com/culture/personal-history/ emilia-clarke-a-battle-for-my-life-brain-aneurysm-surgery-game-of-thrones

Curb Your Enthusiasm. "The Spite Store." Directed by Jeff Schaffer. Written by Larry David. HBO, March 22, 2020

CHAPTER 7

Mikulic, Matej. "Total Number of Registered Clinical Studies Worldwide Since 2000." Statista, February 2, 2021. https://www. statista.com/statistics/732997/number-of-registered-clinical-studies-worldwide/

Pioli, Mariana. R., Alessandra MV Ritter., Ana Paula de Faria., Rodrigo Modolo. "White coat syndrome and its variations: differences and clinical impact." *Integrated blood pressure control*, 11, (2018) 73–79. https://doi.org/10.2147/IBPC.S152761

Shire. "Rare Disease Impact Report." Accessed December 16, 2020. globalgenes.org/wp-content/uploads/2013/04/ShireReport-1. pdf.

Wang, Philip S., Patricia A. Berglund, Mark Olfson, Ronald C Kessler. "Delays in initial treatment contact after first onset of a mental disorder." *Health services research* vol. 39,2 (2004): 393-415. doi:10.1111/j.1475-6773.2004.00234.x

CHAPTER 8

TEDxTalks. "Amy Morin: The Secret of Becoming Mentally Strong." December 4, 2015, video. https://www.youtube.com/watch?v=TFbv757kup4&t=3s

TEDxTalks. "Jake Tyler: 'I'm Fine'—Learning to Live with Depression." Feb 13, 2018. Video. https://www.youtube.com/watch?v=IDPDEKtd2yM

World Health Organization. "Depression." Accessed January 2, 2021. https://www.who.int/news-room/fact-sheets/detail/depression

Wang, Phillip S., Sergio Aguilar-Gaxiola, Jordi Alonso, Mathias C. Angermeyer, Guilherme Borges, Evelyn J. Bromet, Ronny Bruffaerts, Giovanni de Girolamo, Ron de Graaf, Oye Gureje, Josep Maria Haro, Elie G. Karam, Ronald C. Kessler, Viviane Kovess, Michael C. Lane, Sing Lee, Daphna Levinson, Yutaka Ono, Maria Petukhova, Jose Posada-Villa, Soraya Seedat, J. Elizabeth Wells. "Use of mental health services for anxiety, mood, and substance disorders in 17 countries in the WHO world mental health surveys". *Lancet (London, England)*, 370(9590), 2007. 841–850. https://doi.org/10.1016/S0140-6736(07)61414-7

CHAPTER 9

Centers for Disease Control and Prevention. "Loneliness and Social Isolation Linked to Serious Health Condition." Accessed January 13, 2021. https://www.cdc.gov/aging/publications/features/lonely-older-adults.html

Cigna. "Loneliness is at Epidemic Levels in America." Accessed January 13, 2021. https://www.cigna.com/about-us/newsroom/studies-and-reports/combatting-loneliness/

Fox, Susannah, Maeve Duggan. "Health Online 2013." *Pew Research Center.* January 15, 2013 https://www.pewresearch.org/internet/2013/01/15/health-online-2013/

McLeod, Saul. "Maslow's Hierarchy of Needs." *Simply Psychology,* December 29, 2020 https://www.simplypsychology.org/maslow.html

Smee, Sebastian. "You Might Think You Know Frida Kahlo But You'll Never Understand Her Pain." *The Washington Post.* February 14, 2019. https://www.washingtonpost.com/entertainment/museums/you-might-think-you-know-frida-kahlo-but-youll-never-understand-her-pain/2019/02/14/1509f868-2e4e-11e9-813a-0ab2f17e305b_story.html

EDxTalks "Madeleine Boyson: Chronic Illness and Social Media." June 10, 2016. Video https://www.youtube.com/watch?v=JhSb4h-PQtM

TEDxTalks. "Tiffany Yu: The Power of Exclusion." April 4 2018. Video. https://www.youtube.com/watch?v=qVtDejw8ZBw

World Bank Group. "Disability Inclusion." Accessed January 13, 2021. https://www.worldbank.org/en/topic/disability#:~:text=Results-,One%20billion%20people%2C%20or%20 15%25%20of%20the%20world's%20population%2C,million%20 people%2C%20experience%20significant%20disabilities.

CHAPTER 10

Benjamin Gardner, et al., "Making health habitual: the psychology of 'habit-formation' and general practice." *The British journal of general practice : the journal of the Royal College of General Practitioners, 62,605, (2012): 664–666.*

Boyles, Salynn. "100 Million Americans Have Chronic Pain." *WebMD.* June 29, 2011. https://www.webmd.com/pain-management/news/20110629/100-million-americans-have-chronic-pain#1

Diabetes UK. "First Use of Insulin in Treatment of Diabetes on This Day in 1922." Accessed January 18, 2021. https://www.diabetes. org.uk/about_us/news_landing_page/first-use-of-insulin-in-treatment-of-diabetes-88-years-ago-today#:~:text=Insulin%20 was%20discovered%20by%20Sir,than%20a%20year%20or%20 two.

Gardner, B., Phillippa Lally, Jane Wardle, J. "Making health habit-ual: the psychology of 'habit-formation' and general prac-tice." *The British journal of general practice : the journal of the Royal College of General Practitioners, 62,605, (2012): 664–666.* https://doi.org/10.3399/bjgp12X659466

Kripalu Center for Yoga & Health. "Insight Meditation for Calmness and Clarity." Accessed January 25, 2021. https://kripalu.org/presenters-programs/insight-meditation-calmness-and-clarity

Roser, Max, Esteban Ortiz-Ospina, and Hannah Ritchie. "Life Expectancy," Our World in Data. October 2019. https://ourworldindata.org/life-expectancy

World Bank Group. "World Development Indicators." Accessed January 18, 2021. http://datatopics.worldbank.org/world-development-indicators/

CHAPTER 11

Blue Zones. "History of Blue Zones." Accessed January 13, 2021. https://www.bluezones.com/about/history/

Cleveland Clinic. "Here's What Happens When You Don't Get Enough Sleep." Accessed January 29, 2021. https://health.clevelandclinic.org/happens-body-dont-get-enough-sleep/

Felton, Kathleen. "This Italian Village Has 300 People Over 100 Years Old." *Health*. March 13, 2021 https://www.health.com/mind-body/this-italian-village-has-300-people-over-100-years-old

Harvard T.H. Chan School of Public Health. "Doctors Need More Nutrition Education." Accessed January 13, 2021. https://www.hsph.harvard.edu/news/hsph-in-the-news/doctors-nutrition-education/#:~:text=%E2%80%9CToday%2C%20most%20 medical%20schools%20in,obscene%2C%E2%80%9D%20Eisenberg%20told%20NewsHour.

Johns Hopkins University. "The Science of Sleep: Understanding What Happens When You Sleep." Accessed January 29, 2021. https://www.hopkinsmedicine.org/health/wellness-and-prevention/the-science-of-sleep-understanding-what-happens-when-you-sleep

Payne, Cheryl, "The Most Basic and Powerful Way to Connect to Another Person is to Listen." Mind Journal. Accessed January 26, 2021. https://themindsjournal.com/the-most-basic-and-powerful-way-to-connect-to-another-person-is-to-listen/

Tri-City Medical Center. "The Sad Desk Lunch." Accessed January 29, 2021. https://www.tricitymed.org/2017/05/sad-desk-lunch-infographic/

CHAPTER 12

Moore, Peter. "The High Cost of Cancer Treatment." *AARP*, June 1 2018 https://www.aarp.org/money/credit-loans-debt/info-2018/the-high-cost-of-cancer-treatment.html

Schiff, Pam. "I'm Thankful She Never Lost Hope," Cranston Herald, November 25, 2015. https://cranstononline.com/stories/im-thankful-she-never-lost-hope,107509

CHAPTER 13

United Ostomy Association of America. "What is an Ostomy." Accessed January 27, 2021. https://www.ostomy.org/what-is-an-ostomy/

CHAPTER 14

National Center for Chronic Disease Prevention and Health Promotion. "Chronic Disease in America." Accessed February 8, 2021. https://www.cdc.gov/chronicdisease/resources/infographic/chronic-diseases.htm.

O'Neill Hayes, Tara, Serena Gillian. "Chronic Disease in the United States: A Worsening Health and Economic Crisis." *American Action Forum.* September 10, 2020 https://www.americanaction forum.org/research/chronic-disease-in-the-united-states-a-worsening-health-and-economic-crisis/#:~:text=Direct%20 Costs,-The%20health%20care&text=Annually%2C%20direct %20health%20care%20costs,person%20without%20a%20 chronic%20disease.

CONCLUSION

Weatherspoon, Deborah. "Box Breathing." *Healthline.* June 17, 2020 https://www.healthline.com/health/box-breathing

Made in the USA
Las Vegas, NV
04 May 2021

22473155R00105